Advice

from

college

students

who've

been

there —

and lived

to tell

the tale

MASTERING
(& succeeding with)
THE JOB HUNT

Printed on ♲ recycled paper

Presented by
MasterCard International Incorporated
2000 Purchase Street
Purchase, New York 10577
To order additional copies, please call 1-800-JOB-8894

Cover and text design by The Sloan Group

Illustrations by Scott Russo

Photographs by Patrick McNamara

Compilation of text by Christy Lane of BKG Youth

Concept development and management by
Nancy J. Hemenway
Vice President, MasterCard International Incorporated

A portion of the proceeds from the sale of this book goes to the American Marketing Association Collegiate Activities Division.

Dedication

MasterCard International sponsored the development of this book as a tribute to young people everywhere. We hope you will find it useful during your job hunt. *Mastering (& succeeding with) The Job Hunt* is a part of the MasterCard "Master Your Future" series of programs designed to help young people achieve their personal and financial goals.

MasterCard thanks all of you involved in the development of the book. Your hard work and dedication will make many young people smarter about the job search. May you all have very successful futures.

Preface

Kent Findwerk and Anita Job recently graduated from reputable colleges. After four years (more or less) of hard work and substantial financial investment, the two grads were ready to begin their careers: they put together résumés, invested in "interview" suits, searched through the classifieds, and pounded the pavement. After investing considerable time and effort in their respective job searches, Kent and Anita were rewarded with their first career positions . . .

As rejection letters from "real" employers continued to mount, Anita wondered how she would explain to family and friends that the only use she was making of her finance degree was when she "cashed out" each evening. And Kent feared that his future in psychotherapy might be limited to the over-21-and-imbibing crowd. What had they done wrong?

Their respective futures were looking somewhat dim. If only Anita and Kent had gotten some solid advice from people who had been there . . .

ForeWord

The seed for *Mastering (& succeeding with) The Job Hunt* was planted by students two years ago when MasterCard International sponsored the American Marketing Association (AMA) Collegiate Marketing Challenge, an annual forum through which student members of the AMA are invited to compete in developing a comprehensive marketing plan for a business or nonprofit organization. In the first year of MasterCard's sponsorship, the task confronting competitors was straightforward: to develop effective strategies to market the MasterCard® brand to college students. During the competition—in which several teams independently chose "Master Your Future" as the title of their proposed marketing plans—it became evident that the topic of most concern to students was their ability to find a job after college. According to competitors, helping students to prepare for employment upon graduation was one of the most useful services that could be provided.

When MasterCard decided to sponsor the subsequent competition, it adopted the goal of structuring the Challenge in such a way as to give students what they wanted—and needed. Although competing teams traditionally have submitted detailed marketing plans in response to a specific real-life case study (complete with strategic and tactical plans), entrants were asked instead to develop personal marketing plans for obtaining employment in a difficult job environment. The participating students—and their counterparts nationwide—were, in essence, the "product" to be taken to market.

In total, 29 collegiate marketing teams from across the country rose to meet the challenge of "How to Market Yourself in a Difficult Job Environment." In preparing their marketing plans, teams conducted exhaustive searches of secondary sources; evaluated industry and market trends; interviewed students who were in the process of launching their job searches, recent graduates in the midst of their searches, new hires, career placement officials, and employers; and conducted quantitative research. Teams then used this information to develop personal marketing plans that addressed all aspects of marketing oneself in the job market, from choosing a profession to conducting the actual job search. It is upon these submissions—which, in total, reflect hundreds of hours of research and the direct input of hundreds of student competitors—that the core of *Mastering (& succeeding with) The Job Hunt* is based.

To further ensure that *Mastering (& succeeding with) The Job Hunt* meets the needs of today's job hunters, MasterCard sponsored two surveys. The first—intended to measure the needs (and anxiety levels) of those approaching the job search—was completed by more than 2,000 juniors and seniors, representing a variety of backgrounds and majors from colleges and universities across the country. The second survey, sent to 429 college placement officers and 183 corporate employers, had two objectives: 1) to learn what the job market will be like this year and in the near term, and 2) to gain a basic understanding of the do's and don'ts of the job hunt in today's market. The results of the surveys enabled us to broaden the scope of the book by including the views of students in a variety of majors and the insights and experiences of professionals on both sides of the job-search equation.

Finally, 10 student editors representing colleges and universities across the country converged in New York City for an intensive editorial review of *Mastering (& succeeding with) The Job Hunt*. Their comments and recommendations were essential in refining the many elements of this book into an original work that should be of practical use to all college students and graduates who are entering—or trying to enter—the job market.

Mastering (& succeeding with) The Job Hunt is real job-search advice for college students, from college students who have taken the time 1) to assess the plethora of advice and information that's out there, 2) to select that which they deemed most helpful, and 3) to compile it into the most useful format possible. Chapter by chapter, the book will walk you through the many aspects of the job search itself, from making the "right" decisions concerning courses and in-school opportunities that could impact your future employability, to determining which career path to pursue, to that magic moment when you accept a position. It even contains advice on what to do after your job search. In each step of the development of the book, MasterCard's overriding goal has remained constant: to discover anything and everything that might help college students to be better prepared for, and more successful during, the job hunt. To further assist you in making a smooth transition from academia to the world of work, we have included a special section on managing your personal finances during the interim between college graduation and employment.

In the coming months, you will no doubt be faced with difficult decisions. It is our sincere hope that *Mastering (& succeeding with) The Job Hunt* will give you the useful information you need to be successful in both preparing for and conducting your job hunt, as well as in your future career. Good luck!

MasterCard.
It's more than a credit card.
It's smart money.™

–Gary J. Flood, Senior Vice President
MasterCard International Incorporated

–Nancy J. Hemenway, Vice President
MasterCard International Incorporated

In developing *Mastering (& succeeding with) The Job Hunt*, the authors held fast to the ideal of creating a self-study course that would guide fellow travelers safely (and intelligently) through their respective job hunts. The course isn't easy. As you develop personal strategies for meeting each challenge, take solace in the knowledge that you are benefiting from the advice and experience of countless job hunters who have traveled this perilous road before you and lived to tell the tale.

Christy Lane
Vice President
BKG Youth

Acknowledgments

Special thanks to Christy Lane of BKG Youth, who spent countless hours organizing the student submissions into a manuscript, and then devoted more time ensuring the student editor comments were incorporated into the book. Christy's expertise with the youth market was invaluable in the development of *Mastering (& succeeding with) The Job Hunt.*

We would also like to thank Ginny Shipe, director of the Collegiate Activities Division of the American Marketing Association (AMA), for her creative insights and contributions in developing and coordinating the AMA Collegiate Marketing Challenge itself—and for permitting us to draw on her talents during her continued involvement as a valued member of the editorial review board.

Thanks also to Josephine Czochanski, director of brand development at MasterCard International, who managed the book development through its many phases—including production, promotion, and distribution—with contagious enthusiasm and unparalleled attention to what distinguishes a great book from one that is merely good.

We would also like to thank Barbara Schulte, director of brand development at MasterCard International, who was instrumental in forging the relationship with the American Marketing Association and who demonstrated an ongoing commitment to the evolution of the challenge and development of the book.

The judges of the AMA competition finals—Gerry McGrath, vice president of human resources staffing for MasterCard International; June Rogoznica, editor of *Careers and Colleges* magazine; Roxanne Hori, associate director of placement for Northwestern University's Kellogg School of Management; and Sybil Stershic, president of Quality Service Marketing—devoted many hours to evaluating written submissions and judging the oral competition. We are grateful for their hard work.

We would like to thank the student competitors, whose efforts not only made this book possible, but also enlightened MasterCard as to the importance of making such information available to all college students. A complete list of contributors, including information on finalists and winners, can be found at the back of the book.

Table Of Contents

Chapter 6

Chapter 7

Chapter 8

Chapter 9

Chapter 10

Chapter 11

Introduction
A MESSAGE
FROM THE STUDENT EDITORS

Job hunting in the '90s may not be easy, but it's not impossible, either. If you've been feeling discouraged by such headlines as "Job Prospects Bleak," "Corporations Cutting Back on Campus Recruitment," and "Grads Battling It Out for What Few Jobs Remain," we have two words of advice: Don't be. By picking up *Mastering (& succeeding with) The Job Hunt*, you've already given yourself an advantage in this increasingly competitive market.

Welcome to the world of job hunting, '90s style, in which there are two keys to finding a decent job: 1) you must market yourself intelligently, and 2) you must be committed to investing the requisite time and effort into the job search. This book will teach you how to do the former and will motivate you to do the latter because it contains step-by-step, practical advice from hundreds of college grads across the country. By reading this book, you'll reap the benefits of their many successes—and avoid repeating their mistakes.

As you proceed through this book, keep a few things in mind:

First and foremost, **a job search these days takes time.** Don't expect to land your dream job in a couple of weeks or even months. This is not to say that it can't happen, but simply that you should be emotionally prepared to stick it out over the long haul. Financially speaking, not everyone will be able to hold out for their dream job, of course, but managing your financial resources wisely throughout your search will help you to make ends meet until you get that first paycheck.

Second, **attitude is just as important to a productive job search as organization;** it's vital that you guard against negativity and despair. A little bit of stress serves as a good motivator, but it's important that you present yourself as enthusiastic—not desperate.

Finally, **remember to look at the job search as an opportunity rather than a chore.** Even in the worst of times, there are plenty of positions out there waiting to be filled. Once you've defined your dream job, go for it! Convince yourself that you will excel in a certain position, and you'll have gone a long way toward convincing prospective employers of that as well.

Good luck from the student editors!

Kurt Apen
University of Pennsylvania
Economics and Marketing

Jamie Bubier
Wellesley College
History and Psychology

Kimberly Chrisman
Stanford University
English

Roger Fan
Brown University
Sociology and Economics

Greer McPhaden
Columbia University
English

Julie Neenan
University of Michigan
English and Pre-Medicine

Savitha Reddy
Northwestern University
Communication Sciences and Disorder

Sean Ryan
University of California, Santa Cruz
Earth Science and Geology

Brian Shanahan
Georgetown University
International Business and Marketing

Matt Waller
Vanderbilt University
English and Communications

IU

Chapter 1

Self-Assessment:
To Thine Own Self Be True

In today's fast-paced world, it is all too easy to lose one's identity, to lose sight of one's dreams and ambitions. Separating yourself from the competition in the job market involves knowing who you are and what you want to become.

—University of Colorado at Boulder

Self-assessment is an examination of one's own interests, skills, abilities, experiences, education, values, strengths, and weaknesses. In other words, it means figuring out who you are, what you want, and what you've done. You can probably surmise that this process is one of the most important aspects of the job search, because it determines the direction in which you want to focus your efforts. What you will come to realize is that it is also one of the most challenging aspects of the search, because the success of any self-assessment technique is inherently dependent upon your ability to be completely honest with yourself. For a select few, self-assessment will come relatively easily; those of you with concrete goals and a clear vision of how to achieve them are off the hook. For those of you who are somewhat less directed or driven, it will be more difficult.

We'd like to say that all you need to develop a foolproof Grand Plan is the first 12 pages of this book and a half-hour of focused thinking. However, since the foundation of this chapter is honesty, we may as well be straight with you: most likely, you won't complete your self-assessment by the end of today, tomorrow, or even next month. The good news is, you don't have to. In fact, the most successful self-assessment is a continual process, because your vision of where you want to be should be constantly adapted to your changing desires, interests, and skills, and to the world's changing opportunities.

That said, the goal of this chapter is to get you in touch with the person that you are today. You don't have to make all your life decisions in a single sitting, but the sooner you get the career ball rolling in a direction that reflects your goals, the better. This is your life; be in control of it.

Who You Are

Given the effort that goes into identifying and pursuing each job opportunity, you don't want to spend valuable time and energy courting a company or position only to discover that it doesn't meet your career objectives. Knowing who you are—in terms of skills, goals, and personality strengths and weaknesses—will not only provide a focus for your job search, but will also better prepare you to assess the employment opportunities that come your way.

When completing the following self-assessment exercises, in whole or in part, you should keep three very specific goals in mind:

1) To become familiar with your strengths and weaknesses. This information will help you to determine both the professions for which you are best suited and—for those of you a bit further down the self-assessment path—which of your abilities are a solid match with your intended profession. For example, if you identify poor communication skills and shyness as weaknesses, you are probably not suited to working in public relations. However, this is not to say that if public relations is the career path you want, you should not strive to reach your goal. You just have to be willing to work very hard to overcome your weaknesses in order to achieve your objectives.

2) To explore your personality traits. Such knowledge can be vital when it comes time to choose a career path or a specific work environment. If you are a team player and enjoy working in groups, for example, a position in advertising may be attractive. However, if you are a solo player who works best when answering to a single boss, a position as an accountant might be a better choice.

3) To examine your personal and ethical values. You will be happier if the career path you choose and the company culture you enter are compatible with your moral and ethical values. For example, if you, as an engineer, are committed to thinking green, you may want to think twice before signing on as a designer of plastics. On the other hand, you may view the job as an opportunity to influence a particular manufacturer to create products that are made of recycled plastics or are recyclable (or both). The goal is to give some forethought to potential conflicts of interest before you are confronted with the problem.

With these three goals in mind, you're ready to begin your self-assessment.

Exercise 1: PUT IT ON PAPER

Writing is a magic act that lends an aura of permanence, validity, and order to the otherwise random thoughts that fill our minds. Because it's so hard to hide from the realities of the written word, one of the most effective ways to initiate the self-evaluation process is to draw a line down the middle of a sheet of paper; on one side, list all of your strengths, and on the other, list all of your weaknesses. To refine your list, ask your family, friends, and professors to give you their honest and objective opinions. It is very important that you not get insulted or defensive if they tell you things you don't want to hear. No one is perfect, and the sooner you are aware of your weaknesses, the sooner you can improve upon them.

Exercise 2: PUTTING THE FUN IN FUNERAL

If you prefer a more creative approach to self-assessment, don't despair. A management professor at the University of Cincinnati suggests that you write your own obituary. This approach may seem a bit morbid, but if done right, it can produce accurate results. Start by reading obits in *The New York Times* or another major paper. Once you spot someone who seems to have led a particularly interesting life, read the article thoroughly. Next, sit down and write your own "ideal" obituary. It should include all of the important feats you would like to have accomplished before you die, as well as any interesting things you would like to have done in your life. Next, write an abbreviated obituary that includes only those things you had hoped to accomplish by this point in your life. Now compare the two. According to the management professor, "If you are satisfied with your [abbreviated] obituary, you are probably on your way to accomplishing what you want out of life." If not, now's the time to make some adjustments. Remember, too, that as with other self-assessment techniques, this works only if you are honest with yourself.

Exercise 3: THIS IS NOT A TEST (NOT REALLY)

If all this soul-searching has led you down a well-traveled path to a familiar dead end, consider approaching your self-assessment from a different angle. As a college student or recent grad, you may feel quite despondent at our suggestion that you take yet another test, but for those who are genuinely stuck (or simply curious), a visit to your campus career development office may be just the spark you need. These centers typically are staffed by career counselors who can administer what's known as a self-assessment test. Authored by such testing experts as Meyers-Briggs, Strong-Campbell, and Frederic Kuder, many self-assessment tests measure five distinct psychological traits: intelligence, achievement, aptitude, interest, and personality. Although these tests are not intended to determine which career path you should follow, they can help you narrow the field of possibilities. You may even discover that your characteristics and attitudes make you a perfect fit for a career you had never even considered.

Another option to explore is computerized self-assessment programs, which are also designed to help you plan your career. Utilized by many universities, public libraries, career placement centers, and the military, these programs relieve you of the burden of hours spent combing through catalogs and career books. First the programs ask you questions regarding skills, interests, values, education, and so on. Your preferences and background are then matched with various career options. The System of Interactive Guidance and Information (SIGI Plus), developed by the Educational Testing Service, and DISCOVER, developed by American College Testing, are two such programs.

When viewing the printout that is the end result of such computer-aided self-assessment, it's tempting to accept the information as unalterable fact. You should remember, however, that the results of self-assessment tests are but one tool of self-assessment and are most useful when weighed in conjunction with such relatively unscientific data as your gut instincts. Don't allow test results to deter you from a career you want, or push you into one you don't.

What You Want

More than 70 percent of all employees report that their jobs are unfulfilling, because they haven't distinguished between what they can do and what they are temperamentally fit to do.
—Northeastern State University, University Center Tulsa

Now that you have a better idea of who you are, it's time to determine what you want—from life in general and from your career. If the words "a job, any job" are forming on your lips, think again. You have invested an enormous amount of time, energy, and money to obtain a college degree, and before it's all over, you will probably devote a big chunk of time, energy, and money to your job search. You might as well end up in a position or industry you like.

Whether on a personal or a professional level, determining what you are looking for and establishing important goals along the way will help keep you on track as you move toward your ultimate goal—which is, of course, lifelong happiness. (We leave it to you to determine whether that happiness hinges on fame, fortune, family, or a steady income and lots of free time.) Yes, establishing goals takes time, but wouldn't you prefer to dictate where your career will lead you, rather than allowing outside influences to dictate where you are going?

Each "little" goal along the way—developing your writing skills, learning French, passing advanced accounting—is important because it helps to motivate, provide direction, and facilitate decision making. The sooner you assess your goals, the sooner you'll be able to establish a plan of action that will increase your likelihood of achieving your career goals.

Exercise 4: **THINK IT OVER**

To help determine your career goals, try to answer some of the following questions. Really think about them; you may have stronger opinions about some of these issues than you realize.

- What kinds of working conditions do I want?
- Do I want to work as part of a team or by myself?
- Do I want a nine-to-five job or one in which I can set my own hours?
- Do I thrive in a high-stress atmosphere, or would I prefer something a bit more laid-back?
- Do I want an office position or one that involves travel?
- Do I want to stay in a particular city over the long term, or do I want to relocate?
- What kinds of benefits do I want, and what salary range do I desire?
- Do I want a set salary, or would I prefer to work on commission?
- What would I most like to be doing in my job?
- For whom would I most like to work?
- Are there skills I'd like to attain in order to move toward my final goal?
- Career-wise, where do I want to be in five years? In 10 years?

college students speak ABOUT career GOALS

• **Is it more important to you to get a job that is intellectually stimulating, financially rewarding, or socially responsible?**

Financially rewarding	49.9%
Intellectually stimulating	35.4%
Socially responsible	10.2%

• **With which of the following would you rather graduate from college?**

A really good job	57.9%
A really good education	39.5%

• **Which of the following is most important to you?**

The freedom to pursue outside interests	34.7%
A great job	30.4%
Family time	28.3%

• **If the following jobs all paid $40,000 per year, which one would you choose?**

Management consultant	34.3%
Teacher	22.3%
Investment banker	18.8%
Artist	13.8%
Social worker	7.0%
Surgeon	1.8%

Note: The sum of the percentages will not equal 100 because some participants chose not to respond to a particular question.
Source: MasterCard International survey of more than 2,000 college juniors and seniors (September 1993).

Exercise 5: MOBILIZE

Your next objective should be to get more information on careers in which you're interested and to explore additional career options that might be a good match for your recently defined goals. Your first stop should be your college library and/or career center, both of which house a variety of sources on the types of jobs available. Even after you've exhausted your library's supply of secondary material on a particular career or industry, however, there's at least one more step you should take: go to the source, someone who actually lives the life that you are contemplating. If you aren't acquainted with a psychiatrist or an investment banker or a research analyst or whatever it is you are considering as a career, consult your school's alumni office. Many such offices will put you in touch with recent and not-so-recent grads in your field of interest who can provide you with the personal insights that you may or may not find within the pages of a book. It would also be a good idea to contact a professional society in your field of interest; such organizations may be able to put you in touch with individuals who can answer your questions.

Exercise 6: KEEP DREAMING

One of the most critical errors a college student can make is to let the expectations of parents, friends, and professors determine what job he or she will take. This is not to say that you cannot be happy working in what society deems a "successful" career; but don't give up on a dream just because it seems impractical. As you continue to explore your interests through on- and off-campus activities, don't forget to spend some time researching how you can use your degree to realize your dreams.

What You've Done

The objective of this segment of self-assessment is to reexamine the things you have done with a goal of discovering what you like (and don't like) to do, as well as what you are (and aren't) capable of doing. Charting out just what you've accomplished thus far and the specific skills you have acquired along the way will not only result in a better understanding of the types of things you like to do, but also will help you to determine whether your capabilities are in line with your goals. And a special word to those of you who may be tempted to do this exercise in your head: this chart will be put to good use come résumé-writing time.

The following steps will help you uncover your key experiences and accomplishments.

Step 1: EDUCATION

Using the following format as a guideline, list the names of all the courses you have taken in college, as well as any other in-school experiences or accomplishments. Your objective is twofold. First, you want to remind yourself of all you have learned and achieved, and how those experiences can tie in to a career; second, you want to take a closer look at how you reacted to various courses. (What? You can't remember every class you've ever taken? Not to worry. Stop by the registrar's office and pick up a copy of your transcript. If the course title doesn't jar your memory, perhaps the grade will.) If, on looking back over the years, you discover that you never met a math or economics class that you liked, you might want to rethink your plans to become a financial analyst. Even if you're good at something, there's no point in pursuing it if it brings you absolutely no pleasure.

Name of School: UCLA

Major/Area of Concentration: Political science

Favorite Courses: Political science, English, history, public speaking

Least Favorite Courses: Philosophy, economics, psychology

Relevance of Courses to Career: Developed strong written and verbal communication skills, performed intensive research, excelled in critical analysis, worked well on team projects

Special Projects: Taught adults English as a second language, coeditor of campus paper (gained editing, writing, and leadership skills), organized campus blood drive

Step 2: WORK HISTORY

Assessing your work history will provide you with a clearer understanding of your job skills and strengths. It will also afford you a bounty of information that can be used to answer difficult questions posed by prospective employers later in your job search.

Completing a work history evaluation chart such as the one below will help you to understand your technical background, unique abilities, and the ways in which these skills and experiences may relate to your career aspirations.

WORK HISTORY EVALUATION CHART

Company
Sheister, Crookes & Skinflint

Responsibilities
- Legal assistant
- Worked on computer database
- Created deposition abstracts
- Assisted in preparation of report on legal liabilities of bungee-cord manufacturers
- Assisted attorneys with trial preparation and exhibits

Skills Gained
- Communication and interpersonal skills
- Thorough and precise attention to detail
- Ability to abstract information

Special Training
- LEXIS®/NEXIS® Information Services
- Conformed writing to Harvard "Blue Book"

Step 3: ASSESSING YOUR SKILLS

Evaluating your functional and special-knowledge skills will not only help you to pinpoint the ones you can use to your advantage in your job search, it will also make you aware of any gaps or shortcomings in your job-readiness. Functional skills are your abilities to do such things as teach, solve problems, work well with others, or analyze. In general, they are the skills that you enjoy using and that come easily to you. Special-knowledge skills are acquired through specific education. They include such capabilities as computer ability, market research, legal knowledge, technical know-how, and accounting.

The following is a partial list of skills to get you started. Circle those skills that you believe you have acquired and transfer those that you would like to acquire into the Desired Skills List. If you have or would like to have skills that are not on the list, make note of them in the appropriate column in the space provided.

General Skills List

Desired Skills List

Accounting
Administration
Budgeting
Classifying
Computing
Conflict resolution
Consulting
Coordinating
Counseling
Creativity
Data gathering
Dealing with unknowns
Designing
Editing
Evaluating
Explaining
Financial analysis
Fluency in another language
General business knowledge
Graphic arts
Human relations
Interpreting
Interviewing
Investigating
Leadership
Legal skills
Listening

(continued)
General Skills List   **Desired Skills List**

Managing
Mediating
Monitoring
Motivating
Negotiating
Numerical aptitude
Oral communication/public speaking
Organizing
Persuasion or selling
Problem solving
Processing
Programming
Project management
Recruiting
Researching
Scientific experimentation
Social skills
Supervising
Teaching
Technical skills
Working with precision
Working well with others
Written communication

Additional Skills:

Having identified your general skills, all you have to do now is reel them off during your next interview, right? Not exactly. In the job search, saying you have a particular skill is not enough; you must be prepared to back up your assertions with relevant experience (work, school related, leadership, etc.). For each of the skills you have identified, complete the following:

Acquired Skill:
Proven Ability:

Now take a moment to concentrate on your Desired Skills List. There is no time like the present to start adding valuable skills to your repertoire. Remember: you don't have to learn every skill today, but you should develop a plan of action to ensure that you have acquired as many of these skills as possible before you begin your job search. Get started by completing the following for each desired skill:

Desired Skill:
Plan of Action:

11

Step 4: PROFESSIONAL ORGANIZATIONS

Membership and active involvement in a professional organization indicates to a prospective employer that you are dedicated to your chosen profession. Equally important, the experiences you gained there should help you assess whether it's really a profession to which you want to devote a good portion of your life. As you complete the following chart for each organization, don't forget to note participation in special activities or election to executive offices (both of which demonstrate your enthusiasm and leadership qualities).

Organization:
Activities:
Offices Held:

Step 5: LEISURE ACTIVITIES/INTERESTS

At first glance, what you like to do in your free time may seem trivial and unimportant to your job search. In actuality, the way you choose to spend your free time can serve as a clear indication of which activities you most enjoy and value. If you can translate any of these interests and activities into the world of work, you'll be much more likely to find a job that keeps you happy.

For example, if your favorite things to do in the world are rock climbing and motorcycle racing, you may find life as a bank manager kind of dull. You might discover that you'd prefer the risk taking and high stakes of Wall Street or the creative expression of Hollywood. Your education and aptitudes will, of course, influence your final choice, but when you're considering careers, keep in mind that you're going to be spending years and years at one job or another. You might as well do something you find satisfying.

You may also find that your leisure activities have afforded you skills and experiences that could prove helpful in your job search. For example, as center of your college basketball team, you may have demonstrated leadership qualities that an employer will find attractive. Take a few moments to fill out the following for each activity; it may help you to see your free time in a whole new light.

Leisure Activity:
Skills Acquired:
Supporting Evidence:

Now that you know more about yourself than you thought possible, here's one final tip: Never close the door on self-assessment.

Chapter 2

ob Market Analysis: The Ugly Truth—and Your Best Approach

Unless you're a trust-fund kid or the bearer of a winning lottery ticket, you might want to give some thought right now to how you plan to pay the rent in the years ahead. How does this affect your job search? Well, it may not at all—if your self-assessment pointed you in the direction of lucrative labor. But if the path you're intent on taking seems unlikely to support your desired lifestyle, you may want to give your plan a second look. By taking the time to explore all your options, you could have the best of both worlds: happiness in a career that also allows you to pay the bills. After all, if jobs were only about having fun, we'd call them hobbies.

The Ugly Truth

Chances are, your job search will be conducted in the midst of news headlines announcing corporate layoffs, hiring freezes, and other dismal tidings. But according to the Bureau of Labor Statistics, total employment in the United States is expected to increase 20 percent (an addition of 24.6 million jobs) between 1990 and 2005, and of those projected jobs, 9 million are expected to require a college degree. Which scenario should you believe? Both of them. In reading the fine print, one learns that the projected rate of growth for the years 1990 to 2005 is just slightly more than half that of the previous 15-year period (1975–1990).

What do these numbers mean to you? College graduates entering the labor force in the 1990s and early 2000s are all but guaranteed to face a job market that is significantly more competitive than that faced by graduates in the 1980s. In her article "The Future of Jobs for College Graduates" (*Monthly Labor Review*, July 1992), Kristina Shelley, an economist with the Office of Employment Projections, Bureau of Labor Statistics, explains, "Employment projections for the 1990–2005 period indicate that the average annual openings in jobs requiring a degree will be fewer than the opportunities available in the 1984–1990 period. At the same time, projections of bachelor's degrees by the National Center for Education Statistics indicate that the average annual number awarded is expected to be greater over the 1990–2005 period than for the 1984–1990 span." It doesn't take an econ wizard to figure out the impact of that scenario, but we've included the following chart to make the reality a little more, shall we say, real:

Economics in Action: Supply and Demand of College Graduates

	1984–1990	1990–2005
	(actual)	(projected)
SUPPLY		
New graduates entering the labor force annually	974,000	1,106,000
Other graduates entering the labor force annually*	214,000	214,000
Total annual college graduate labor force entrants	**1,188,000**	**1,320,000**
DEMAND		
Number of jobs requiring a college degree opening annually due to growth or upgrading	767,000	602,000
Number of workers who permanently leave existing college-level jobs annually	197,000	312,000
Total annual job openings for college graduates	**964,000**	**914,000**

* Includes college-educated immigrants, recently discharged military personnel, persons recently released from institutions, and the net increase of those returning to the labor force (primarily women who had stopped work to care for their families).
Source: Office of Employment Projections, Bureau of Labor Statistics.

Despite the gloomy outlook, the majority of college graduates are expected to find college-level jobs. The difference being, whereas eight of every 10 college graduates found jobs that required a college degree during the 1984–1990 period, that ratio is expected to drop to seven out of 10 between 1990 and 2005. And what about the projected 406,000-person annual surplus of college graduates? They will find work, according to the Bureau of Labor Statistics—just not in positions that traditionally require a four-year degree. (Uh-oh.)

college students on JOB earch Anxiety

- **What's the general attitude of you and your classmates regarding the job market?**

Nervous, but hopeful	49.3%
Pessimistic	19.6%
Optimistic	15.3%
Anxious/stressed out	12.1%
Apathetic/blasé	1.3%

- **Do you think you and your classmates have to be more willing to settle for a less-than-ideal job than were students in 1985?**

Yes	68.7%
Don't know	15.5%
No	15.0%

- **Do you think it's going to be easier, the same, or harder for you and your classmates to get jobs than it was for the Class of 1988?**

Harder	76.9%
The same	15.3%
Easier	6.3%

- **Do you think your college is adequately preparing you to succeed in the workplace?**

Yes	71.9%
No	26.3%

- **What do you think are your chances of being employed when you graduate?**

0 percent	.7%
25 percent	8.1%
50 percent	24.8%
75 percent	33.5%
100 percent	24.4%

- **When do you think you will have a job?**

Before graduation	29.8%
Within three months after graduation	33.7%
Three to six months after graduation	22.6%
Six to 12 months after graduation	5.3%
More than a year after graduation	3.0%

- **Have you ever considered going to graduate school just to postpone the job hunt?**

No	61.8%
Yes	21.8%
It will be a fallback strategy if I don't get a job	14.3%

Note: The sum of the percentages will not equal 100 because some participants chose not to respond to a particular question.

Source: MasterCard International survey of more than 2,000 college juniors and seniors (September 1993).

15

Your Best Approach

The point of these seemingly dismal tidings is this: as critical as self-assessment is to your job search, it is not always enough to decide which careers interest you. (If it were, the world would probably be teeming with baseball players, ballerinas, and rock stars.) In today's competitive job market, you must also consider which careers are in demand. You can help improve your chances of being among the "lucky seven" by staying up-to-date on such things as labor force trends, employment opportunities, and expected growth in various regions of the country.

This chapter will help you to do that and will also discuss the specifics of researching particular industries and companies. Yes, we know. It does sound pretty exciting.

LABOR FORCE TRENDS

Our economy—for those of you who managed to avoid econ altogether—is generally divided into two sectors: the service-producing sector and the goods-producing sector. In recent history, an industrial restructuring has resulted in a shift from goods-producing industries to service-producing industries for a number of reasons, including changes in consumer tastes and preferences, legal and regulatory changes, advances in science and technology, and changes in management of businesses. In fact, of the 24.6 million new jobs expected to be created between 1990 and 2005, 23.3 million will be in nonfarm wage and salary jobs—almost all of which are projected to occur in the service-producing sector of the economy. No, this doesn't mean that you'll have to spend the rest of your life saying, "Do you want fries with that?" The service industry goes way beyond hawking hamburgers.

The Service-Producing Sector

For analysis purposes, the Bureau of Labor Statistics divides the service-producing sector into six divisions:
- Transportation, communications, and utilities
- Wholesale trade
- Retail trade
- Finance, insurance, and real estate
- Services
- Government

Within the service-producing sector, the **services** division is expected to account for nearly one-half of total growth between 1990 and 2005. The division's two largest industries, health services and business services, will account for an increase of 6.1 million jobs. Health services encompasses medical technology, home health care, nursing homes, clinics, and hospitals. Business services include personnel, computer, and data processing. Other service industries with strong growth potential are social, legal, engineering, education, and management services.

In the same period, the **wholesale** division is projected to add 1 million jobs, with job growth being stimulated by an increase in exports.

The fastest job growth within the **retail** division is projected to be among apparel and accessory stores and eating and drinking establishments. These two industries are reportedly benefiting from higher levels of personal income and the continued increase in women's participation in the labor force. Overall, 5.1 million jobs are expected to be created within the retail division from 1990 to 2005. Eating and drinking establishments are expected to account for 42 percent of the division, food stores for 13 percent, automotive dealers and service stations for 9 percent, and apparel stores and general merchandise stores for around 8 percent each.

Within the **finance, insurance, and real estate** division, bank mergers and acquisitions, the closing of unprofitable branches, and the installation of additional automated teller machines are expected to limit the demand for additional employees at depository institutions (banks, savings and loans, and credit unions). Nondepository institutions, such as finance companies and mortgage brokers, are expected to fare better. Projected increases in the number of jobs between 1990 and 2005 are 275,000 in nondepository holding and investment offices and 232,000 in depository institutions. The securities and commodities brokerage industry is projected to add about 114,000 jobs between 1990 and 2005. During the same period, an additional 240,000 jobs are projected for insurance carriers, and 221,000 jobs are projected in the insurance agency, brokerage, and services industry. Real estate employment should rise from 1.3 million to 1.6 million.

Within the **transportation, communications, and utilities** division, four out of five new jobs will be created within the trucking industry (410,000 jobs) or the air transportation industry (276,000 jobs) by 2005. Communications, by contrast, began declining in the mid-1980s following the divestiture and reorganization of AT&T. The strongest growth in public utilities will be in water supply and sanitary services.

Employment in the **government** division is expected to increase from 15.2 million to 18.3 million jobs from 1990 to 2005, with more than half of these positions in the public education sector.

The Goods-Producing Sector

The goods-producing sector is divided into three divisions: mining, construction, and manufacturing.

The majority of jobs in the **mining** sector in 1990 were in the crude petroleum and oil field services industry. By the year 2005, it is expected that 40 percent of the nation's oil supply will come from foreign countries (up from 24 percent in 1990). Rising oil prices are expected to increase interest in domestic exploration, and therefore, the employment rate in the oil field services industry is expected to increase slightly. However, when the numbers of jobs in the crude petroleum and oil field services industries are taken together, a loss of 17,000 jobs is expected. A loss of 35,000 jobs is projected in the coal industry.

Although expanding domestic and export markets for American goods is expected to lead to a projected growth of 2.3 percent in real output, technological advances are likely to result in a smaller workforce making more goods. Overall, a half-million jobs are expected to be lost in the **manufacturing** industry between 1990 and 2005.

Construction is the only goods-producing sector with projected job growth, and that is largely due to projections in government spending on additions of or improvements to roads, bridges, and other infrastructure.

Employment Opportunities

In general, employment opportunities for college graduates are expected to outpace those for non–college graduates. The following charts represent the fastest-growing occupations and the occupations with the largest projected job growth. (For a look at projected changes among occupations not listed below, consult "Occupational Employment Projections," *Monthly Labor Review*, November 1991.)

Fastest-Growing Occupations, 1990–2005 (numbers in thousands)

Occupation	Employment 1990	Employment 2005	Numerical Change	Percent Change
Home health aides	287	550	263	91.7
Paralegals	90	167	77	85.2
Systems analysts and computer scientists	463	829	366	78.9
Personal and home care aides	103	183	79	76.7
Physical therapists	88	155	67	76.0
Medical assistants	165	287	122	73.9
Operations research analysts	57	100	42	73.2
Human services workers	145	249	103	71.2

(continued)

Occupation	Employment 1990	2005	Numerical Change	Percent Change
Radiologic technologists and technicians	149	252	103	69.5
Medical secretaries	232	390	158	68.3
Physical and corrective therapy assistants and aides	45	74	29	64.0
Psychologists	125	204	79	63.6
Travel agents	132	214	82	62.3
Correction officers	230	372	142	61.4
Data processing equipment repairers	84	134	50	60.0
Flight attendants	101	159	59	58.5
Computer programmers	565	882	317	56.1
Occupational therapists	36	56	20	55.2
Surgical technologists	38	59	21	55.2
Medical records technicians	52	80	28	54.3
Management analysts	151	230	79	52.3
Respiratory therapists	60	91	31	52.1
Child care workers	725	1,078	353	48.8
Marketing, advertising, and public relations managers	427	630	203	47.4
Legal secretaries	281	413	133	47.4
Receptionists and information clerks	900	1,322	422	46.9
Registered nurses	1,727	2,494	767	44.4
Nursing aides, orderlies, and attendants	1,274	1,826	552	43.4
Licensed practical nurses	644	913	269	41.9
Cooks, restaurant	615	872	257	41.8

Source: Bureau of Labor Statistics.

Occupations with the Largest Job Growth, 1990–2005 (numbers in thousands)

Occupation	Employment 1990	2005	Numerical Change	Percent Change
Salespersons, retail	3,619	4,506	887	24.5
Registered nurses	1,727	2,494	767	44.4
Cashiers	2,633	3,318	685	26.0
General office clerks	2,737	3,407	670	24.5
Truck drivers, light and heavy	2,362	2,979	617	26.1
General managers and top executives	3,086	3,684	598	19.4

Occupation	Employment 1990	2005	Numerical Change	Percent Change
Janitors and cleaners, including maids and housekeeping cleaners	3,007	3,562	555	18.5
Nursing aides, orderlies, and attendants	1,274	1,826	552	43.4
Food counter, fountain, and related workers	1,607	2,158	550	34.2
Waiters and waitresses	1,747	2,196	449	25.7
Teachers, secondary school	1,280	1,717	437	34.2
Receptionists and information clerks	900	1,322	422	46.9
Systems analysts and computer scientists	463	829	366	78.9
Food preparation workers	1,156	1,521	365	31.6
Child care workers	725	1,078	353	48.8
Gardeners and groundskeepers, except farm	874	1,222	348	39.8
Accountants and auditors	985	1,325	340	34.5
Computer programmers	565	882	317	56.1
Teachers, elementary	1,362	1,675	313	23.0
Guards	883	1,181	298	33.7
Teacher aides and education assistants	808	1,086	278	34.4
Licensed practical nurses	644	913	269	41.9
Clerical supervisors and managers	1,218	1,481	263	21.6
Home health aides	287	550	263	91.7
Cooks, restaurant	615	872	257	41.8
Maintenance repairers, general utility	1,128	1,379	251	22.2
Secretaries, except legal and medical	3,064	3,312	248	8.1
Cooks, short order and fast food	743	989	246	33.0
Stock clerks, sales floor	1,242	1,451	209	16.8
Lawyers	587	793	206	35.1

Source: Bureau of Labor Statistics.

SALARIES

The following listing—compiled from the *Jobs Rated Almanac*, the *American Almanac of Jobs*, and the *Encyclopedia of Careers* (vol. 2)—cites the academic majors that were most in demand in 1992, and their approximate starting salaries:

Major	Starting Salary
Accounting	$23,222
Biology/biological sciences	$26,946
Business administration/management	$26,598
Chemical engineering	$29,256
Chemistry	$24,524
Civil engineering	$30,608
Computer engineering	$27,900
Computer programming	$21,822
Computer science	$23,664
Electrical/electronic engineering	$35,650
Elementary education	$17,238
Finance/banking	$19,620
General engineering	$27,900
Hospitality/hotel/resort management	$18,595
Industrial engineering	$35,010
Language (interpreter)	$38,000
Management information systems	$23,664
Marketing/retailing/merchandising	$16,000–$21,000
Math/actuarial science	$32,155
Medical technology	$18,838
Psychology	$28,800
Sales	$ 9,265
Secondary education	$17,238
Taxation	$17,004

If your chosen field of interest is not on the list, it doesn't mean that such salary information isn't available. Sources you can consult to determine the average starting salary in a given field include surveys conducted by trade and professional associations, the *College Placement Council Salary Survey*, *American Almanac of Jobs and Salaries* (available in your local library or bookstore), professionals who work in your field of interest, and recent graduates who have accepted positions similar to those in which you are interested.

REGIONAL VARIATIONS

Regional variations in population growth also affect the demand for goods and services, as well as the availability of occupations and industries. These population shifts reflect higher or lower birth rates and the movement of people seeking new jobs or retiring. The population in the West, the country's fastest-growing region, will increase 19 percent between 1990 and 2005. During that same time span, the population in the South is expected to increase 15 percent, the population in the Northeast is expected to increase 4 percent, and the population in the Midwest is expected to remain the same.

Northeast: Job competition is fierce, but there is a strong demand in high-tech industries related to health care, as well as in health care–related research, primary care, medical technology, and insurance.

Southeast: This region is struggling in the areas of banking, real estate, and retail. The strongest positions in this area are in sales and marketing.

Southwest: Although the impact of downsizing has been felt most in this region, unemployment in sections of this area is lower than in other parts of the country. Positions are available in every industry.

Northwest: Companies in this area of the country are also downsizing and trying to relocate as many employees as possible. The strongest industries are aerospace and its suppliers, real estate, and recreation and travel services.

Tax Dollars at Work:
Career Information Sources from the U.S. Government

Most libraries—especially those on college campuses—have a special section that includes career information, and releases from the federal government are some of the best references out there. If the following publications are not in your library, you may purchase them directly from the U.S. Government Printing Office, Washington, DC 20402.
- The *Occupational Outlook Handbook* is published every year by the U.S. Department of Labor. It provides detailed and up-to-date information about hundreds of careers. This valuable information includes a description of the nature of the work, working conditions, the number of people in a field, qualifications and training needed to enter each field, prospects for advancement, the job outlook for the upcoming decade, and average earnings.
- The *Occupational Outlook Quarterly* includes up-to-date articles on changes and trends in the job market, emerging occupations, and—not that you wouldn't surmise this from the title—occupational outlooks.
- The *Dictionary of Occupational Titles* categorizes every job in the American economy.

22

INDUSTRY BY INDUSTRY

One of the best ways to analyze the job market is to break it down into the industries in which you are interested. The more specific you can be, the more relevant the job market figures will be to your search. Using the reference materials available in your library, you should be able to determine such information as current employment trends, the extent of opportunities in each industry, the leading companies in the industry, and how many businesses exist in certain geographic areas.

The best place to start your search is by locating the Standard Industrial Classification Code (SIC) for your industry of interest. The SIC system is based on the federal government's *Standard Industrial Classification Manual*, which is the standard index to company classification nationwide. After selecting the proper SIC, cross-reference the following publications to learn specific information about companies of interest to you: *The Million Dollar Directory*, *Value Line*, *U.S. Industrial Outlook*, and *Standard & Poor's Industry Surveys*.

This information will also help you to determine which companies are most stable. For example, economically sound firms will tend to expand, hiring more employees than do weak ones. A job opportunity analysis work sheet, such as the one provided below, will help you get started.

Job Opportunity Analysis Work Sheet

Industry Description: _____

SIC(s): _____

Geographic Area: _____

Number of Firms: _____

Companies to Contact:

_____

_____

_____

_____

COMPANY BY COMPANY

The search for the right job is not easy, but anything you can do to more clearly define and focus your job search will be beneficial in the long run. The more you know about particular companies, the more efficient you will be at targeting companies in which you are interested and eliminating those in which you are not.

The first step is to learn the company's background. All public companies must make corporate and financial information readily available to the public.

Your search should begin in the library, with the following objectives:
- When was the company established, and by whom?
- What are the parent companies/subsidiaries, if any?
- Is this company in an advancing/stable industry?
- Who are the company's chief competitors?

Additional issues for consideration, which may require a bit of creative research, include
- Quality of management
- Financial soundness
- Quality of production services
- Ability to attract, develop, and keep talented people
- Use of corporate assets
- Value of long-term investments
- Innovation
- Community and environmental responsibility

If you have narrowed your field of interest to a specific department within the company, you should attempt to get an idea of how the department is run. The basics include the following:
- What is the highest-ranking position, and how many of those positions are there?
- What are the lower divisions, and to whom do they report?
- How do the individual departments in the company conjoin and work as a whole?

Knowledge of these basic facts will help you to determine whether you are interested in pursuing a career with a particular company. And should the time come, such knowledge will serve you well during your interview with the company.

THE SMALL-COMPANY ADVANTAGE

In hopes of maxing out their first-year earning potential, many grads set their sights on Fortune 500 powerhouses and neglect to explore the increasingly lucrative small-company advantage. There is certainly nothing wrong with starting out in the big leagues, but it may be worth your while to do some scouting in the minors as well. In the first place, corporate downsizing and industry fluctuations mean that large companies are no longer the bastion of job security they once were. More importantly, they don't necessarily offer the best opportunities. In fact, when *Inc.* magazine identified the 500 fastest-growing private companies in fourth quarter 1992, they turned out to have an average of 145 workers.

Why are so many of the smaller companies thriving? Two primary reasons are that they serve a niche market and that they are being hired by some of the corporate "giants" to handle work that, prior to downsizing, was done in-house.

Although you will most likely discover that researching a small company is somewhat more challenging than researching a large one (primarily because small companies are often privately held and, as such, are not required to produce publicly available annual reports), you may discover that the extra effort is well worth your time. Although it's true that small companies are more prone to going under, it's equally true that the lack of a large bureaucracy makes advancement easier and allows for more varied experience in different areas of the company. And if you do decide to join a large corporation down the road, the experience you gained at a small company may allow you to get further faster than if you had begun in the big leagues.

THE '90s

A marketing graduate of the University of Cincinnati advises, "Like the old saying goes, it's a jungle out there." This graduate, who was in the job market for nearly nine months before finding a job, notes that many college graduates do not realize that to land the job of your dreams, you must be willing to make some compromises. In this case, the compromise meant starting at a lower pay rate than expected.

Career success in the '90s will be a challenge because of the changing market environment. College students and recent grads are adapting to these realities by lowering their sights and compromising on such issues as salary, field of interest, and geographic location. Others are choosing to work toward graduate degrees that may or may not give them an edge in the next go-round. And most distressing for some grads, moving back in with one's parents during the transition period is now more typical than taboo. In addition to doing your homework about prospective employers before an interview, there are several things that you can do to better your chances of obtaining a desired position:

- Prepare a strong résumé.
- Harness and add to your strengths; minimize your weaknesses.
- Be willing to work your way up.
- Be willing to start at a lower salary than expected.
- Be willing to relocate.
- Above all, remain confident and do not get discouraged in your job hunt.

The following chapters will tell you more than what to do—they'll tell you how to do it.

Chapter 3

Demystifying the Job Search: What to Do and When to Do It

Remember that the difference between successful and unsuccessful job hunters is not some external factor like "a difficult job environment," but the way the job search and career planning are conducted.

—Virginia Polytechnic Institute and State University

Too often, college grads assume that a diploma is all it takes to get a job. In reality, your diploma simply puts you in the running—it takes a good deal of thought and planning to get your foot in the door. The best advice we can give you in this competitive market is to plan ahead. Freshman year is none too soon to start laying the groundwork.

If you're planning a career in a technological or scientific field, for example, you may discover that some employers have a very specific idea of what courses they want their prospective hires to have taken. It would certainly help if you knew this before your last quarter in school.

In addition to course work, companies very often have a well-defined list of standards against which applicants are measured. Those of you who have your hearts set on corporate America, for example, should know that America's top companies define the perfect hire as having the following qualifications: a business degree and exposure to other disciplines; experience starting a company and expanding it many times over, as well as extensive exposure to the business environment; proven ability as an innovator in customer service and product quality; excellent written and oral communication skills; a track record of leadership; and a thorough understanding of the global economy.

Now, any of you who actually have all those qualifications should probably put down this book and go solve the health care crisis or balance the national budget. Everyone else should start breathing again and realize that recent grads are cut a whole lot of slack. After all, it would have been kind of hard to run and expand a company, what with exams and parties and all that.

What companies do look for among the recently released is evidence of the following characteristics: respectable grades, enthusiasm, flexibility, problem-solving ability, a high energy level, and maturity. These traits enable an employer to tell that a job candidate is goal oriented, adaptable, and committed.

The following recommendations are based on the personal experiences of soon-to-be and recent grads, as well as the employers who wield the you-get-the-job wand. If you take their advice, you'll at least be giving yourself an edge.

What to Do: Professional Development

Thomas Jefferson once said, "I'm a great believer in luck, and I find the harder I work the more I have of it." There is definitely some luck involved in finding a job. The best we can do is to try to increase our chances of getting a lucky break—which means devoting a lot of time and effort to this endeavor.

—University of Virginia

1) There's more to a good education than getting good grades, but whether you're applying for grad school or seeking employment, it's important that you **get good grades.** For those of you who've been doing well all along, don't slack off now. This doesn't mean you must have a perfect grade point average (GPA), but you might as well strive for one. If you have academic problems that cannot be addressed by professors, you should join or form a study group, seek tutorial help, or—as your very last option—drop the class. For better or worse, prospective employers will view your grades as a reflection not only of your abilities, but also of your drive to succeed. This is not to say that you should spend every waking moment in the library, but when a party is competing for essential study hours the evening before a major exam, remembering the academic rule of thumb may strengthen your resolve: it's easier to get a good grade in a course than it is to explain a bad one (this goes for parents and prospective employers alike).

By excelling in a variety of courses, you can show potential employers that you not only have a wide range of skills, but that somewhere along the line you did very well in something you didn't even like. Doing well in everything demonstrates an admirable work ethic, something most employers are in the market for.

Hot Tip: The second semester of your senior year is too late to repair significant damage incurred by your GPA during the previous seven or more semesters. However, all is not lost. When the moment of truth arrives and you are finally asked to place a numerical value on the success of your education, be aware that you can report your GPA in at least two ways: overall/cumulative or GPA in major.

2) When evaluating the skills of a particular job candidate, many companies pay special attention to written and oral **communication skills**.

It is vital to be able to write a meaningful document and carry on an intelligent conversation. A Seaboard executive who refers to written and oral communication skills as the "softer" skills says that they are one of the first things his company looks for in a prospective employee. In an ever-changing work environment, being articulate and well-versed is increasingly important. Communication skills are also necessary during your job search: written skills get you in the door by enabling you to develop a high-quality résumé and cover letter, and a person with strong verbal skills will be more successful in an interview.

If these areas aren't exactly your forte, sign up for classes that will strengthen these skills. English, speech, journalism, communications, and acting are all viable options. Though your previous method of choosing classes may have entailed the automatic elimination of any course that was rumored to require even the minimum communication skills, as an enlightened future job-seeker, you should now flock to classes that require a variety of written and oral assignments.

If you want to improve these skills without putting your GPA on the line, explore not-for-credit educational opportunities offered by a local community college or community center.

3) Because you will most likely need one or more recommendations when you begin your initial job search, it is advisable to **cultivate mentor relationships**

(the more the better) with professors or professionals in your field of interest. The key to having rewarding mentor relationships is to establish them as early in your college career as possible. (Hint: if you don't have one in the works, the time to get started is now.) A good way to improve your personal visibility and marketability is by working part-time on professors' research projects or papers. If a paid research position is not available, *be prepared to volunteer*.

In addition to helping you score a letter of recommendation, mentor relationships give you a chance to meet significant people within your discipline and broaden your networking circle. A long-term relationship with your professor(s) may also prove useful to you long after you've landed your first career position.

4) You are no doubt aware that our world is fast becoming a "global village." As someone who will live and work in this interrelated environment, it is prudent to **think and act globally,** and increase your market appeal by taking the following steps:

• Stay abreast of current events, both foreign and domestic. A simple suggestion: read the newspaper. Fifty cents is a small price to pay for information, and many local papers—as well as such nationally respected newspapers as *The New York Times* and *The Wall Street Journal*—offer a discounted rate for students. A variety of papers are available in college and public libraries.

• Enroll in a course related to international business or foreign policy. It's a small world, and a general knowledge of the ways in which various countries (and the academic institutions, companies, and people within them) relate to one another will serve you well as technological advances continue to increase the likelihood of your direct participation in such interaction.

• Learn a foreign language. *¿Habla español? Sprechen sie Deutsch? Parlez-vous français?*

Even without the skills necessary to understand those questions, the message is clear: foreign languages are becoming an increasingly valuable asset. From a nurse working in an inner-city hospital to a banker in charge of Mitsubishi's U.S. account, foreign-language skills can make your job easier and can make you more attractive to employers. If language courses aren't required for your chosen curriculum, take the initiative: *aprende español, lernen sie Deutsch, aprendez-vous français,* or learn any language that interests you and that may be relevant to your field of interest. There's more than one way to learn a language: register for a class, become friends with an exchange student, or opt for the do-it-yourself method by borrowing instructional language tapes from a library or by purchasing a set at a bookstore.

• Pursue international educational and travel opportunities. Whether participating in a university-coordinated semester in Europe, signing up for a three-week stint at an anthropological dig in Guatemala, or spending a summer on a self-guided backpacking trip through Asia, such travels help to transform you into a—dare we say it?—more "well-rounded" person by providing direct exposure to, and immersion in, the cultures of the world beyond the United States. Take advantage of such opportunities (or create your own) whenever possible.

29

5) The information age is here to stay. As you prepare for your career, it is all but essential that you **acquire computer knowledge.**

In order to be competitive, you must ensure that your skills meet or exceed those of competing job candidates. At a minimum, take a basic word processing class or stop by your campus computer center for an introduction to the essentials. From this starting point, you may consider further training in basic programming, desktop publishing, or simply mastering the software packages used most often by professionals in your field of choice. According to a professor of business computer systems at New Mexico State University, the two programs most frequently used in the business world are Lotus 1-2-3 for spreadsheets and WordPerfect for word processing. If you're hoping to be employed by a company that speaks "Mac," the programs to know would be Microsoft Excel and Microsoft Word. (P.S. Most computer programs come with tutorials that teach you the basics.)

6) A skill that may or may not be developed in a classroom environment is leadership, but that doesn't mean that you can't **enhance your leadership skills** during college. Investigate clubs and organizations to discover what they have to offer and whether their activities match your interests. Then, choose those activities that will provide you with an opportunity to develop managerial and leadership skills. The key to making these groups work for you is active involvement; simply showing up for the yearly group photo won't do much for your personal—or professional—development. Participation in clubs and organizations also can help you develop motivational, organizational, and interpersonal skills that may not be emphasized in the classroom. In addition, clubs can introduce you to various fields and ideas that might assist you in choosing your career path.

Another option to consider is getting involved in off-campus volunteer opportunities. You can become a better leader and improve your management skills, for example, by doing such things as coaching a youth hockey or soccer team or coordinating volunteers at a shelter for the homeless or at a hospital.

7) Students who **participate in internships** develop skills and gain work experience that helps them to determine whether a particular career path is right for them. Internships typically are arrangements between businesses and colleges/universities that allow students to gain academic credit for on-the-job experience, usually lasting an academic semester or term. Although some internships are paid and/or for credit, don't overlook opportunities that provide nothing more than experience. What you learn may be far more valuable than a stipend or course credit.

In recent years, corporate giants such as General Motors, AT&T, and IBM have enthusiastically hired thousands of interns. For some lucky students, this experience can lead to an offer of a permanent position after college. For example, the employment director at Allstate Insurance, has set a goal of hiring 40 percent of Allstate's 1995 entry-level staff from its intern program. The Kraft General Foods manager of staffing and organization, says, "We view the internship as a recruitment tool. Good internships take a lot of the supervisor's time and attention. However, the payback is substantial when we are successful in bringing on board an intern who is familiar with our company, our product, and our culture." IBM's director of employment and recruiting, explains, "It is in our interest to have people who have already worked for us in our company."

Most for-credit internships are coordinated by academic deans or career development/placement officers in conjunction with human resources directors. Applicants typically provide a résumé, cover letter, transcripts, and a writing sample. If your school does not have contacts with a firm in your field of interest, don't be afraid to approach companies on your own or to ask the career development counselor to assist you in your search.

Hot Tip: Although internships are a valuable form of professional development for undergraduates, they aren't just for college students anymore. Many recent graduates are using them as stepping stones to gain the experience or certainty of direction they need before launching their postgraduation job search.

A 1993 graduate of Colorado College, spent his collegiate summers working as a writing tutor at a camp for gifted and talented students. He so enjoyed this experience that his first-choice career option was to put his English degree and writing skills to use as a teacher in a private high school. But things don't always work out the way one plans them. Even though he had his first interview in November of his senior year, he was still unemployed in May. Fortunately, he had a backup plan. In December of his senior year, he read in *Harper's* that the magazine had internships available for college students and recent graduates. Since he had served as news editor of his college paper, he was intrigued by the internship description and decided to apply.

He was offered (and accepted) one of the positions, but there was one catch: the positions were unpaid. As a graduating senior, he would naturally have preferred to draw a salary instead of depleting his savings, but he had a choice to make. It was a tough decision, but he definitely viewed it as an investment, he admitted that "New York is not the cheapest place in the world to live," but he didn't regret his decision at all.

As an intern, he not only determined that he would like to pursue a full-time opportunity as a member of the editorial staff of a consumer magazine, he also gained practical experience in such tasks as fact checking, reading unsolicited manuscripts, and "some clerical things" that will help him reach his goal.

For information on internships with companies ranging from *Harper's* to the American Legislative Exchange Council, from the Petrified Forest National Park to the Federal Reserve Bank of Chicago, consult *Internships 1994: Over 30,000 On-the-Job Training Opportunities for Today's Job Market* (Peterson's Guides, 1993).

8) **Externships** (sometimes referred to as *shadowing*), which are usually available through college and university career centers, are an opportunity for students to spend a short period of time (typically a week) in a career field of their choice. The extern program at the University of Virginia, in operation for 15 years, is the largest of its kind in the United States. Three times each year (January, March, and

summer break), students are placed with sponsors in their field of choice. The objective is to give students an opportunity to gain firsthand knowledge of a career field and to provide the sponsor with unpaid assistance for a week. As an extern, you would be expected to provide your own housing and would not be monetarily compensated for time spent with a sponsor; however, you would gain valuable work-related experience and the opportunity to network in your career field. Externships also represent a prime opportunity to conduct informational interviews and to gain firsthand knowledge of the job routine in your field of interest. If you've narrowed your career choice to two or three fields of interest, an externship can also be a great way to "career-shop."

As with internships, don't be discouraged if your university does not have a formal externship arrangement in the field of your choice. Try to identify someone in your school's career planning and placement office who has some experience in the area or, if all else fails, take the initiative and contact a potential company or individual directly.

9) **Explore cooperative education** as a way to tie college experience and work experience together. This program allows students the opportunity to alternate between academic work and actual in-field experience (usually on a semester or quarterly basis). The rotation provides a welcome change from traditional academic programs and helps ensure job placement after college. Unfortunately, not every college provides students the option of cooperative education. Also, some schools provide this opportunity only for business students. If it is an option at your school, check it out. Through the integration of study and work, cooperative education promotes career awareness and develops career skills. Job-search skills are introduced as early as freshman year, and co-op students continue to benefit from ongoing experience in résumé preparation, interview techniques, decision-making skills, and developing a network of future contacts. Unlike internships, most co-op programs pay participants for their work. This means that, in addition to work-related experience, students earn wages that can help finance their college education. What a great way to earn a college degree!

One of the great things about co-ops is that you can use them to learn about a field of interest that is "in your backyard," or you can use them to explore opportunities with companies in other cities. Consider these two examples of students at Merrimack College, located in North Andover, Massachusetts:

• Anthony Velardo, a finance major, gained insight into his field of study through a co-op position at the Boston Stock Exchange. In this position, he was able to apply his academic knowledge of the fundamentals of stock trading on the floor of an actual exchange.

• Julie Oriola, a marketing major, was selected from among applicants at more than 200 colleges and universities nationwide to participate in the Walt Disney World College Program in Orlando, Florida. Julie's experience at Disney's MGM Studios, along with weekly business seminars, taught her what it takes to become successful in the business world. In her co-op program, Julie also had the opportunity to interact with many foreign-exchange students and to learn a lot about their cultures.

For more information on schools that offer co-op education opportunities, contact the National Commission for Cooperative Education, 501 Stearns Center, 360 Huntington Avenue, Boston, MA 02115; (617) 373-3770.

10) No matter what college or university you attend, **volunteer** work provides an excellent opportunity to attain useful skills. Secondly, it shows prospective employers that you are willing to sacrifice (remember, "volunteer" means no pay) in order to gain experience. Last summer, Julie Neenan, a pre-med senior at the University of Michigan, accepted a nonpaying position conducting molecular oncology research with the University of Cincinnati Medical School. Although such positions are usually reserved for medical students, Julie learned of the opportunity by networking with the father of children she used to baby-sit. (For more information on effective networking, see chapter 5.) Of her decision to volunteer, Julie says, "In the long run, I knew I would get more out of the experience than whatever I'd make in tips as a waitress." Her decision paid off: she has been offered a paid position for next summer and will receive credit for her research in published articles, both of which will go a long way when Julie applies to grad school. As an added bonus, Julie was able to get valuable advice on the do's and don'ts of applying to medical school from coworkers who had recently survived the process.

There are a number of routes through which you can volunteer. For example, if you are interested in politics, you could work at your local party headquarters, or if you are interested in a medical or social services career, you could be a "candy striper" at a local hospital. Even if you volunteer with an organization that is unrelated to your field of study (e.g., Big Brothers/Big Sisters), you will still be demonstrating commitment, responsibility, and character, three traits that weigh heavily in employers' evaluations. As more companies become aware of their social responsibilities to the communities in which they are based, employees are encouraged to donate their time and talents to such community projects as early intervention for troubled youth, literacy programs, and drug- and alcohol-abuse programs. They're pleased to find prospective employees who will enthusiastically volunteer under the company banner.

11) The résumés of recent college grads often look very much alike in terms of education and work credentials. The task before you, therefore, is to make yourself stand out from the crowd. You could use neon pink paper and attach a nude photo of yourself to your cover letter, but what we recommend is a tad more subtle: **learn something new and different.**

The idea is to broaden your base of experience by participating in such things as cultural groups, intramural and team sports, a social or professional fraternity/sorority, curriculum-oriented clubs (such as the American Marketing Association), social clubs, musical or drama groups, and hobby clubs. If you aren't content to be a "joiner," you can challenge the status quo by starting your own business, staging a rally, organizing a sit-in, starting a new club, or establishing a new periodical.

Columbia University senior Greer McPhaden chose to carve a niche for herself in an existing student organization, Columbia Student Enterprises. As an English major, Greer knew that the majority of her academic course work would not touch on the finer principles of effective management and strategic financial planning. She wanted to gain practical business experience that would enhance her knowledge base, her résumé, and her bank account. During her freshman year of college, Greer worked for a student-run business that delivers such things as flowers, exam survival packages, and birthday cakes to Columbia students. As a sophomore, Greer set her sights on the manager's position. Just to be considered for the job, she was required to develop a budget and a business proposal, in which, among other changes, she recommended that the organization make a marketability-enhancing name change from Columbia College Care to Columbia Special Delivery.

Greer got the job and, as manager, was responsible for hiring and firing employees, creating sales brochures, determining what to sell and at what price, and in her words, "dealing with evil vendors who would change their prices in the middle of the year for seemingly no reason." After two years as manager, Greer says that being the boss not only taught her the ins and outs of business relations, it made her a better employee: "As manager of a student organization, you don't pay yourself a salary until you have cleared a certain profit margin, but employees get paid on a regular basis. So I know how frustrating it can be when you are paying people who don't want to work. Now I feel too guilty to slack off on the job when someone's paying me."

For information on establishing a business of your own, contact the Center for Student Entrepreneurship, Wichita State University, Wichita, KS 67260; (316) 689-3000.

In addition to making your résumé uniquely yours, extracurricular activities can give you experience in some important areas. Note the following examples:

Activity	Demonstrated Characteristics
Scouting	Perseverance and achievement
Competitive sailboat racing	Teamwork and competition
Volunteer firefighting	Accepting challenges, teamwork, decision making under pressure
Extensive travel, both domestic and foreign	Open to new experiences
Videography, photography, radio production work	Creativity
Community service, fund-raising	Organizational skills and enthusiasm

12) Whether you are interviewing with a recruiter on campus, attending a business dinner, or taking part in an internship, there's no doubt about it: *your actions will be observed.* One's ability to **understand corporate etiquette** is an increasingly important factor in developing one's marketability. According to Joanne Mahanes, coordinator of career development and assistant dean of the University of Virginia's College of Arts and Sciences, you should choose a role model—someone who demonstrates the professional conduct you want to emulate. Identify the qualities that make this person stand out in your mind, and take steps to develop those qualities in yourself.

If your school does not offer a corporate etiquette seminar, you can learn about these topics through a variety of self-help books and videotapes on the market today. You will want to focus on how to make proper introductions and business greetings, how to participate in social conversations, and what constitutes proper table manners. For those intent on exploring career opportunities abroad, it would be particularly helpful to read books aimed at helping American business travelers avoid faux pas with foreign clients and partners. Deportment and politeness certainly aren't everything, but they continue to be an integral part of the preparation necessary to conduct an effective job search.

When to Do It: A Career-Planning Time Line for Professional Employment

The following sample itinerary is intended to demonstrate how an ideal job search would be carried out. We realize, however, that different people focus on the job search at different times in their college careers. If you are reading this book at the start of your freshman year, your parents must be very proud. For those of you who are being measured for a cap and gown next week, don't despair; you'll just have to do a bit of catch-up work. No matter how late you think you may be in terms of getting started, tomorrow is even later. After reading through the following time line, take a deep breath and develop your very own accelerated time line to get you on track. Whatever you do, start today.

Freshman Year

Freshman year is a time for experimentation. First and foremost, learn everything you can and *enjoy yourself*. Although you should get involved in school activities and organizations, your entire year should not be devoted exclusively to establishing an active social life. As Mom or Dad will be quick to remind you when grades are in: "Remember why you are in college."

- For those of you listed among the critically undecided, make the most of your freshman year by taking as wide a variety of classes as possible. You may discover new interest in subjects that you had sworn off at the high school level; you may even discover interest in subjects that you didn't know existed.
- Seek an unpaid internship that affords you professional work experience, personal contacts, and (optimally) the potential for future employment or a co-op opportunity.
- Consider using the college work-study program to your best advantage by finding an on-campus job that can also serve as a résumé item. Consider these examples: working in the career development office affords you a wealth of contacts and training in employment-search techniques; working in the registrar's office offers extensive training in customer service; working in admissions offers a bird's-eye view of marketing; working in the alumni relations office affords personal contacts and public relations skills. All of these positions require communication abilities and interpersonal skills, both of which are vital to careers in a variety of fields.
- Take a self-assessment test to help you discover career positions that are a good match for your aptitudes, interests, values, attitudes, and ambitions.

- Consider starting a notebook in which you will keep track of extracurricular activities, interview results, jobs held, etc. This will serve as an invaluable resource when it's time to prepare your résumé.

Summer Before Sophomore Year
- Participate in a summer work-experience program or secure employment related to your general field of interest.

Sophomore Year
If you didn't do so in your freshman year, it's time to declare a major. Don't panic: it's not an unalterable decision, but organizing your academic life is a bit easier if you get it "right" the first time. Narrow your considerations to the best of your ability and, if you still can't make up your mind, seek advice from professors, career counselors, friends, and family members. Most importantly, listen to yourself.
- Explore leadership opportunities in campus organizations with which you have become involved.
- Develop a college-oriented résumé and begin to collect letters of recommendation from previous (and current) employers.
- Consider unpaid internships or volunteer positions as a means of building professional experience and personal contacts.
- Seek professionally oriented part-time or full-time employment. Many students hold nonprofessional jobs, such as pizza delivery or restaurant work. While this work earns income, it will not help you a whole lot in the postgraduation job search. By sophomore year, attempt to hold jobs that are more professionally oriented.
- Begin to develop unique knowledge or skills that are in demand in your field of interest. These may include desktop publishing, writing, a second language, etc.
- If your college offers a study-abroad program, it is most often for one or both semesters of the junior year. Should your college not offer a program abroad, check to see whether they accept transfer credit from other institutions. Those who are seriously considering this experience should look into the application process early to ensure that no deadlines (or by extension, opportunities) are missed. If you want to go, but don't have the financial resources, ask your collegiate adviser whether scholarships are available. You may be pleasantly surprised.

Summer Before Junior Year
- Hold part- or full-time professionally oriented jobs or participate in an internship or summer work-experience program. Continue to update your résumé and collect letters of recommendation.

Junior Year

If you've been putting it off, now is the time to focus on your career objectives and your résumé. School-sponsored career workshops—on subjects ranging from résumé writing, to interviewing tips, to dressing for success—are critical at this time. Take advantage of all such opportunities.

- Remain employed in a professional setting and pursue a cooperative education (co-op) experience.
- Other options might include a government internship, teaching assistantship, and/or resident assistantship. Different schools offer different programs, so be sure to check out your options with your adviser or the career development office.

Junior and Senior Years

If you know that you are going to be looking for a job that begins immediately after graduation, be prepared to spend much of your junior and senior years planning for your search and assessing your career goals. (But don't spend so much time planning your search that you run out of time to put it into action.) Investigate companies that are of interest to you so that you will be aware of interviewing opportunities.

Even those of you who have your minds set on graduate school should go through the senior year job-search process. We aren't espousing negativity, we're just advising a reality check. Do not stop looking for a job until you are accepted by an academic institution you want to attend—and you are positive you have the finances to attend. Anything could happen, so it is important to have a back-up plan if needed.

- Halfway through your junior year and into your senior year, you should begin to alter your résumé so that it is geared more toward professional employment and less toward college-level employment.
- Arrange informational interviews.
- Collect and/or update your letters of recommendation.
- Seek secondary data regarding various career options. Visit your school's career placement office and library.
- Determine whether your job-search focus will be geographically based or opportunity based or both (i.e., are you determined to live in a certain area of the country, regardless of the quality of opportunities available, or are you willing to go anywhere if the opportunity is right?). If you have a preference as to where you want to live after graduation, gather telephone directories and subscribe to newspapers from those areas to keep abreast of employment trends and opportunities in the chosen areas. If, instead, you choose to focus on leading firms in your discipline, begin to gather specific information about the companies, initiate correspondence, and arrange informational interviews whenever possible.

- Attend your college's career day. This is one of the few occasions when company representatives will gather specifically to meet entry-level job candidates.
- If you have decided to send a "general" mailing of letters and résumés to as many companies as possible, you should set a target mailing date of late winter/early spring of your senior year.

Senior Year

- Pick up a calendar of events from your career development office that keeps you informed of on-campus interviews, informational interviews, mailings, etc.
- Set a goal: "I expect to be employed by [date]." Now say it like you mean it.
- Make any necessary postgraduation plans. Some students opt to relocate, travel abroad, work in a resort area for the summer, etc.
- Establish a plan (financial and otherwise) for the period after graduation and before you have found permanent employment.
- Count down to graduation.

A Special Note to the Previously Preoccupied: Initiating Your Job Search

If you've been putting off beginning your job search because the whole thing seems overwhelming, take comfort in the fact that you're not alone. The key to overcoming your hesitation is to focus on taking one step at a time. The following tips will help you to get started:

Procrastination Busters

Divide your work into manageable units. When a task is so large that it intimidates you, it's easy to procrastinate. Break your task down into smaller ones; as you complete each phase, you'll gain a sense of accomplishment and progress.

Start small. Begin with the easy tasks that aren't very time-consuming. You may find it helpful to use checklists.

or

Do the most difficult part first. If you get the hardest part of a project out of the way first, you'll feel as though you can cruise through the rest of it.

Set goals. Check out chapter 6 for some really great goal-setting ideas.

Use the "n" word when you need to. Don't get caught up in distractions while trying to do the project.

Set reasonable deadlines. Plan for unexpected problems.

Reward yourself. Rewards can be powerful motivators. When you finish a large task, treat yourself in some way, no matter how small.

Allow yourself to fail. Remember: nobody is perfect. Just do the best you can.

Accentuate the positive. Try to keep activities in a positive light, regardless of how boring or tedious.

Start. Waiting for the "right" time can defeat you. Set a time and get started.

Chapter 4

Résumés and Cover Letters: Important Keys for Opening Locked Doors

Résumés and cover letters are often the only basis companies have for deciding who gets in the door for an interview and who gets a polite thanks-but-no-thanks note. As such, these may very well be the most important one-pagers you will ever write, but don't let that intimidate you. Presenting oneself effectively on paper is not an easy process for most people, but it's not an impossible one, either. Like conducting a job search, writing your résumé and cover letter(s) will require quite a bit of what parents and grade-school teachers refer to as "your undivided attention." The good news is, it's never too late to make needed improvements—both in yourself as a qualified job candidate and in the format and style of the documents themselves.

Guidelines for
Preparing an Effective Résumé

The best résumé is the one that gets you the interview; all the others are just learning experiences.

—Northeastern State University, University Center Tulsa

A résumé is a summary of your educational and employment background and any other qualifications you have for a particular position. A poorly written résumé, or a résumé that looks amateurish, will most likely be sorted into the round file (a.k.a. wastepaper basket) within seconds. How do you ensure that your résumé is among those earmarked for callbacks? Provide the employer with the needed information in the order and language that make it easiest to read and understand, while establishing your strengths and advantages over the competition. There is no one way to write a résumé, but there are guidelines that are helpful.

If you've successfully completed your self-assessment, you should have a decent written—or, at the very least, mental—outline of your skills, work-related experience, and career goals. If this information exists only in your head, it's time to put pen to paper. (Note: If any or all of these things remain unclear to you, go back to chapter 1 and try again. You may find it useful to review the sample résumés at the end of this chapter so you have a clearer idea of what your self-assessment should yield.)

Your first step in creating an effective résumé should be to visit your university's career development and placement center. In addition to housing a library of information on résumé writing, your placement center is home to advisers who can provide you with résumé-writing tips and critiques. Some placement centers even offer résumé-writing seminars.

In preparing your résumé, you have two options: to have it done professionally by a résumé-writing service or to prepare it yourself. If you choose the professional route, expect to pay around $60 for assistance in editing a self-compiled rough draft of your résumé and no less than $100 for the services of someone who will conduct a one-on-one interview with you and then write your résumé from scratch. Be advised, however, that the word *professional* may be misleading in this case. Professional résumés rarely contain mistakes, but they tend to be very structured, generic in nature, and difficult to personalize. Not surprisingly, such résumés are also easily identified by prospective employers, who may conclude that you were either unable or unwilling to do the work yourself. A self-created résumé is more likely to stand out from the crowd.

When writing your résumé, think in terms of the benefits you offer an employer. By comparing your skills (identified in your self-assessment) with those desired in your field of interest (identified in your job-market analysis), it should be easy to determine what qualities you would bring to the position. But having the right qualifications is only part of the equation. To land an interview, you must be able to communicate your qualifications effectively on paper; this includes making informed decisions regarding language usage, organization, and presentation. Don't forget: it's not only what you say, it's how you say it.

LANGUAGE

Whether describing a paid position, volunteer work, or involvement in a student organization, the following guidelines will lend clarity and strength to your message:

1) Be results oriented. Today's employers are looking for accomplishments. Sure, you may have been president of a student organization, but what did you do as president? What relevant business and interpersonal skills did you gain that will be applicable to your career? For example:

Instead of
> President, American Marketing Association, September 1993–May 1994
> –President of 60-member organization
> –Presided over officer group

Write
> President, American Marketing Association, September 1993–May 1994
> –Raised membership 50 percent, from 30 to 60 members
> –Motivated officer group to accomplish all goals and objectives

2) Use active verbs. Passive verb constructions—as well as phrases such as "responsible for" and "duties included"—tend to be boring. You should strive to use vivid language, without succumbing to any latent tendencies to overdramatize. A proven method for creating a more interesting (and, thereby, more effective) résumé is to start each sentence with an action verb.

Instead of
> Responsible for preparation of the sales tax report each month for my superiors

Write
> Prepared monthly sales tax report for management

Instead of
> In charge of organizing and taking care of three banquets for groups
> of 50 or more people

Write
> Organized and directed three banquets for groups of 50 or more people

43

Consider incorporating these and other action words into your résumé:

achieved	developed	managed
acted	directed	operated
administered	edited	organized
advised	established	originated
analyzed	executed	planned
approved	formed	prepared
assisted	formulated	presented
budgeted	generated	promoted
calculated	handled	recommended
clarified	headed	researched
conducted	implemented	revised
constructed	increased	scheduled
contracted	initiated	supervised
coordinated	integrated	transformed
created	interacted	utilized
defined	led	verified
designed	maintained	

3) Quantify your achievements whenever possible. For example, "supervised others" can be made more specific (and more impressive) by stating "supervised three junior sales associates."

4) Incorporate a brief explanation of your activities whenever necessary.

Example:

Instead of
> *Recipient of John Doe Scholarship*

Write
> *Recipient of John Doe Scholarship for Exemplary Public Speaking Skills*

Instead of
> *President of Kappa Epsilon Gamma Fraternity*

Write
> *President of 80-member Kappa Epsilon Gamma Fraternity, which is dedicated to undertaking education-oriented public service projects*

5) Use professional, work-oriented language. This is not an exercise in glorifying the most menial and mindless of tasks. Instead, you should view it as an opportunity to showcase work-related skills that may not be obvious at first glance. For example, if you worked as a prep cook in the kitchen of a local restaurant, it's easy to surmise that you mastered the art of chopping vegetables. Though this is a skill that may one day thrill your spouse, it's probably not all that important to a prospective employer outside the restaurant industry. What he or she is more likely to be interested in is the fact that you were promoted from assistant prep cook to prep cook in only two weeks.

Example:

Occupation:
Waitress
Instead of
Waited on tables
Write
Ensured customer satisfaction through prompt, cordial service

Occupation:
Shoe salesperson
Instead of
Took inventory
Write
Took charge of procurement and receipt of merchandise and inventory control

6) Use the specific vocabulary of the industry wherever possible. To acquaint yourself with the acronyms, accepted abbreviations, and buzzwords that will help to give your résumé a familiar feel to the employer, read trade magazines specific to your industry and make note of words that come up during your informational interviews. After all, you are trying to demonstrate that you are prepared to work in the industry.

A soon-to-be graduate interested in pursuing a career in publishing, for example, will not only be keeping abreast of industry trends by flipping through the pages of *Editor & Publisher*, but will also be learning such things as that SPJ stands for the Society of Professional Journalists, that roto-magazines are newspapers' rotogravure-style magazine supplements, and that the difference between a mass-market paperback and its cousin, the trade paperback, is its size.

7) Be grammatically correct and check your spelling. The last thing you want to do is distract prospective employers with grammatical inaccuracies (e.g., using *it's* instead *of its*). Furthermore, in today's world of computer technology, there is no excuse for a misspelled word. Most new typewriters and computers are equipped with a word processing function that checks spelling. If you have questions about grammar or punctuation, ask someone who knows the answer. It's the surest way to save your résumé from sudden death. SPEAKING OF SUDDEN DEATH, NEVER, EVER MISSPELL WORDS OR NAMES. IN FACT, ACCURATE SPELLING IS SO CRITICAL THAT WE'LL SAY IT AGAIN, IN BOLD: **NEVER, EVER MISSPELL WORDS OR NAMES**. Last but not least, be sure to have as many people as possible (friends, relatives, etc.) proof the final product.

ORGANIZATION

Having identified relevant skills and experience and determined the most effective way to communicate this information to a prospective employer, it's time to get organized. We recommend using a simple résumé format, such as the one described below. According to human resources professionals, an evaluator does not want to spend time figuring out how to read your résumé; he or she wants to be able to find information quickly.

Though there are literally dozens of ways in which you can organize your résumé, the essential components are the same. You will most likely want to incorporate each of the following aspects into your résumé, in approximately the same order as they appear below. These descriptions should give you a good idea of how best to distribute your qualifications among each section. The "Presentation" section of this chapter, which includes sample résumés, will give you tips on layout and formatting.

Bear in mind, too, that reverse chronological order is generally regarded as the most effective presentation for the various sections of your résumé. When listing relevant experience, for example, you would list your most recent position first, followed by the next most recent, etc. Ideally, your most recent experiences will be those most closely related to your career objectives.

Heading

Your name, address, and phone number should appear prominently at the top of your résumé. Students who will soon be graduating may want to list two addresses: a school address (listed as "Current Address") and their parents' home address (listed as "Permanent Address"). Be sure to indicate on what date you will be available at your permanent address.

Make sure that the address and phone number you give will be valid for the duration of your job search. After one failed attempt to contact you, an employer may just move on to the next applicant. If your address does change, be certain to leave a forwarding address; calls may come months after you've distributed your résumé, and even if by that time you already have a job, establishing additional contacts in your field is always useful.

If possible, the phone number(s) listed should be equipped with answering machines or forwarded to an answering service. Including a fax or E-mail number may also help an employer reach you.

Hot Tip: If you're interested in a "corporate-type" job, the message that is on your answering machine during your job search should not feature your favorite Dead or rap tune as background music. This doesn't mean that your message should be devoid of personality, but it should be brief and professional (e.g., "You have reached the answering machine of Anita Job. Thank you for calling. Please leave a message after the tone, and I will get back to you as soon as possible."). Don't forget to advise roommates and/or siblings that your Great Job Search has commenced, and—if it's not common practice in your home—be sure to ask or beg or bribe them to answer the phone professionally and to take *accurate messages*.

If you don't want to invest in an answering machine, research voice mailbox services in your area. These services, which typically cost around six dollars each month, ensure that potential employers connect with a personalized message and that they are able to leave a private message for you. If you do activate a voice mailbox, be sure to list that phone number on your résumé. Finally, if you plan to be out of town for a few days, don't forget to indicate that on your voice mail greeting so that callers who don't hear back from you immediately won't automatically assume that you are negligent in returning your calls.

Objective

An objective is similar to a personal mission statement and, when included, generally follows the heading, because the statement must be specific enough that the prospective employer knows you are focused, but general enough that it doesn't limit your options within a company. Many career counselors, in fact, advise leaving out an objective altogether for two reasons: 1) writing an effective cover letter can serve the same purpose, and 2) the space on your résumé may be better utilized to highlight your experience.

In the event you choose to include an objective, we are including a few examples. To be effective, it is best to tailor your objective to each company or position targeted in your job search.

OBJECTIVE Marketing position, with an emphasis in sales
OBJECTIVE To utilize my corporate fund-raising skills in a not-for-profit setting
OBJECTIVE $100,000 annually, for starters, and a 10–hour work week [we just wanted to see if you were reading carefully]
OBJECTIVE An editorial position with growth potential
OBJECTIVE Microcomputer programming in a network environment

Career-Related Experience

Human resources professionals tell us that relevant work experience (with an emphasis on *relevant*) is one of the most important categories of a résumé. For this reason, we advise emphasizing your experience over your education. We do want to point out, however, that there is no definitively right or wrong order in which to present this information. Only you know the comparative strengths of your experience and education, and you must determine the presentation order that will best suit your needs.

Although lack of career-related experience is a common concern among undergraduates, the good news is that almost all experience, when properly interpreted, can be useful. Refrain from listing obvious duties; instead, list accomplishments and skills gained. (Refer to number 1 under "Language.") Even if you worked your way through college at Burger King, you gained valuable experience in customer relations and interacting with people.

For each position held—be it a part- or full-time job, an internship, a work-study experience, or volunteer work—list dates of employment, name of employer, position, and if necessary, a description of your job. If your job titles are more important than the places of employment, list the positions first and the companies second. If the companies are more impressive than your job (e.g., you worked in the mail room at Merrill Lynch or as an errand runner for the World Wildlife

Federation), then list the company first. Whichever route you take, be sure that you're consistent throughout the résumé.

Students may also want to ask past or present employers for permission to "upgrade" a job title for résumé purposes. Thus, *sales clerk* might become *sales associate*, and *typist/file clerk* might become *office assistant*.

Hot Tip: Be careful not to include a "laundry list" of jobs on your résumé. Choose only those jobs that have provided you with experiences and qualities that employers are looking for. And if you do plan to avoid mention of an employment position, be sure that you don't bring it up during an interview. This will only cause the interviewer to wonder what else you chose not to include.

Example:

EMPLOYMENT UCSB CHEMISTRY DEPARTMENT, Santa Barbara, California
Research Associate, 1990–1991, 1993
- Conducted experiments in strict accordance with written methodologies to originate data used in Professor Pritchard's articles published in the *Journal of American Chemistry Society*

Education

If a review of your recent employment history reveals no career-related positions, it is best to emphasize experience gained through course work. Begin by listing your educational experience first, making every effort to link your academic achievements to your career goals.

The organization of this section varies but should include the college or university you attended, the type of degree conferred, and your date (month/year) of graduation. If you received more than one degree or attended more than one college, state the most recent degree/college first. If you have not yet graduated, write "candidate" after the degree expected.

Example:

EDUCATION **Boston University**
M.B.A. Candidate, Accounting Concentration   1994

Merrimack College
B.S., Finance   1990

or

EDUCATION UNIVERSITY OF CALIFORNIA, Santa Barbara, California
B.A., English Literature, minor in Communications, 1990

Areas of concentration you might wish to list in this section include relevant course work, awards and honors, and foreign-language skills.

Including your grade point average is optional; it should only be added if it will improve your chances of success. If you do include it, you can be selective as to the version you use: cumulative, only classes in major, or only classes in the last two years. If you do not list it, be prepared to submit that information during your interviews.

Lest there be any doubt, information pertaining to your high school educational experience generally has *no place* on your college résumé. The exception to this rule is if you are applying for an internship or summer job at a corporation in which a fellow alum will be influential in the decision-making process. As you begin your official postcollege job search, however, rely on networking to get such potentially decision-swaying information to the source.

Hot Tip: To make your résumé more readable, try rearranging the material under various headings and subheadings. Examples: Professional Experience, Internships, Entrepreneurial Experience, or Additional Experience. Organizing your résumé in a logical way will make the potential employer's task that much easier.

Activities

On many résumés, this section functions as a subsection of the education heading and is limited to participation in scholastic and professional organizations.

A long list of memberships in organizations may look good, but remember that your goal in an interview is to describe active participation or leadership positions that will allow you to demonstrate learned skills. An employer will be much more impressed with your commitment and contributions to a few organizations than with your card-carrying membership in 10. Be prepared also to answer pointed questions during an interview about each of your activities; not being able to demonstrate that you are an up-to-date, active member could prove more harmful to your job search than not mentioning the organization in the first place.

When compiling your list of activities, beware when it comes to organizations and causes, political or otherwise. The more you tell about yourself, the greater the chance that you will mention something that puts you in the discard pile. Therefore, unless you are prepared to risk following your convictions into the thanks-but-no-thanks pile, affiliations and activities should only be mentioned if you are certain that the information will be received favorably. Your job market research, outlined in chapter 2, should help you judge whether your activities are in line with those of the company and its mission. For instance, if you are seeking employment with a company that has a strong environmental position, such as The Timberland Company, you might want to mention your membership in the Sierra Club. This information might best be omitted, however, if the company in question is not a clear proponent of environmental protection. When making these choices, keep in mind, too, that your résumé is being evaluated by *individuals*, not companies. With regard to those activities not directly tied in to your career goals or major accomplishments, it might be more sensible to err on the side of omission in the case of any activity that could be deemed controversial.

Although scholastic activities should be given priority in this section, it is also acceptable to include hobbies that give insight into your personality and might serve to distinguish you from other applicants. Inclusion of such activities also lets the prospective employer know that you are a well-rounded individual. Your enthusiasm for triathlon competition, for example, may indicate to the reader that you are a dedicated and determined achiever.

Hot Tip: If you are struggling with whether to mention a favored cause on your résumé, you may want to reconsider whether you really want to work for the company in question. Although a given corporation's mission statement probably won't match your personal convictions item for item, you may gain more satisfaction working for an organization that supports causes that are close to your heart.

Skills and Interests

To enhance your presentation, we recommend that you list four to six of your strongest and most relevant job-related skills (not hobbies). These might include any computer skills, foreign-language fluency (if you did not mention it under "Education"), licenses, or special training that relate to the job sought. To draw added attention to this information, we recommend listing your skills in column format.

Example:

SKILLS
- Conducting primary and secondary research
- Fact checking
- Line editing
- Working knowledge of PageMaker and QuarkXpress

SKILLS
- Advanced technical/analytical aptitude
- Expert at Lotus 1-2-3 and Microsoft Excel
- Demonstrated skill in scientific and business-related quantitative analysis
- Conversant in Spanish

References

In days of yore, "References available upon request" often appeared as the last entry on a résumé. This is no longer necessary—or even desired—because prospective employers fully expect that you will provide them with such a list should they ask for one. The *only* reason that you might want to include a reference section at the end of your résumé is if you have a reference from a highly regarded and well-known person in your chosen field.

51

The most likely scenario is that you will be asked to include reference information on a written application form as you wait to be interviewed. To demonstrate your preparedness, you may want to construct a reference sheet (see example) that can be presented during job interviews. For each of two to five references, you should include the person's name, title, company name and address, and daytime phone number. To ensure a professional presentation, be sure the paper stock of your reference sheet matches that of your résumé.

As your base of professional contacts increases, your reference sheet can be better tailored to match a particular job. A word of caution, however, as you enlarge the circle of people who will be called upon to speak knowledgeably on everything from your skills and contributions to your personality and work ethic: always inform the people you plan to use as references. There is nothing more embarrassing than listing a reference who does not remember who you are. And even though references are not always called upon, let them know about the position(s) for which you are interviewing, so they can be better prepared for a phone call.

Example:

PROFESSIONAL REFERENCES
OF
MARY PETERS

Gary White, Vice President
Sales and Marketing Department
The ACB Company, Inc.
701 Simpson Avenue
Providence, RI 02903
(401) 555-1999
(Former Employer)

Professor Linda Adams, Faculty Advisor
American Marketing Association
Johnson & Wales University
8 Abbott Park Place
Providence, RI 02903
(401) 555-2000
(Collegiate Advisor)

Presentation

As a recent or soon-to-be college graduate, you should limit the length of your résumé to one page. If you have difficulty paring yours down, consider this: placement experts have suggested that the longer the résumé, the more likely the employer will find cause for rejection.

When making decisions regarding formatting, you should consider tailoring your résumé to the company with which you are seeking employment. For example, if you are interviewing with IBM's corporate communications department, you may want to use a more conservative approach. When interviewing for the same position at Time Warner, however, a more creative approach might be warranted. Remember, though, that the point is to be creative, not inappropriate.

Once you feel confident about the content of your résumé, you may want to consult a professional graphic designer—or at the very least, a friend with an artistic eye—to assist you in developing an effective layout. Professional designers can help get your résumé the attention it deserves by helping you choose from among a variety of formats and typefaces.

The following tips apply no matter what career you are pursuing:

- Do not crowd the paper. Margins at the top, bottom, and sides should be no less than one inch.
- Be consistent—and selective—in your use of **bold**, underlining, s p a c i n g, CAPITALIZATION, +YPE S+YLES, and margins.
- Type your résumé, preferably on a computer so changes can be made easily and often.
- If you are printing your own résumé, be sure to take advantage of laser printers, which will ensure a top-quality print. If you don't have your own laser printer, rent time at a local quick-print shop or your campus computer center.
- Warning: Colored paper may seem an appealing choice, but its lack of versatility may be your undoing. Companies often make photocopies of résumés for distribution or filing. If your résumé is printed on colored paper, the copy may be illegible. To be on the safe side, it is best to use 8 1/2" x 11" heavy white or off-white bond paper.
- For a professional look, use matching paper to type résumés, cover letters, and thank-you letters, and use matching envelopes.
- Do not include

The word *résumé*	A reason for leaving a job
Testimonials	Information on salary
Personal information	A personality profile
Photo	The statement "References available upon request."

- New technology may be making things easier for human resources professionals, but it is also creating new challenges for résumé writers. To more easily identify likely candidates in the early stages of the job search, many of today's larger companies are feeding résumés into databases that will be optically scanned for key words or phrases instead of being read by human beings. If you anticipate that your résumé will be given this treatment, call the human resources department to find out for certain. If the answer is yes, follow these additional formatting guidelines:

1) Forget italics, boldface, and unconventional fonts; they don't scan well.
2) Never send photocopies of your résumé—gray areas will confuse the scanner because of lack of contrast.

3) Along those same lines, stick to white or beige paper.

4) Use lots of technical jargon; the computer is looking for it.

5) Do not go below 12-point type; this also confuses the scanner.

6) Do not fold your résumé; words in creases will not be read.

7) Avoid using a double column—the scanner reads from left to right straight across the page. You'll also want to avoid splitting up key phrases.

FINAL STEP IN RÉSUMÉ PREPARATION

In addition to seeking guidance from many people during the preparation of your résumé, you should have at least three professionals critique the "final" version before you send it out to prospective employers. At this stage, it is important to remember that each of the people you consult is drawing on his or her personal experience. Should your advisers disagree about something, follow your gut instinct. After all, your résumé is a reflection of you, and you must be comfortable with what it says and the way in which the information is presented.

Pages 56 through 60 include five sample résumés. Review them for formatting ideas that best fit your qualifications.

the electronic RÉSUMÉ

The computer is changing the face of the job search. Computer databases are popping up that classify job seekers according to skills, interests, and education. This method benefits job seekers by eliminating potential human bias in the screening for qualifications. On the other hand, critics are quick to point out that diminishing the human factor can lead to an impersonal process. Impersonal or not, it is clear that the computer will be used more and more to help manage and limit the paper flow of the human resources office.

One such database is Operation Transition, a military-operated, automated job-posting and referral service that helps to match veterans with civilian jobs. The purpose of Operation Transition, as with any such database, is twofold: it assists military personnel in finding civilian jobs, while also offering employers a cost-effective recruiting tool.

An option for nonmilitary job seekers is offered through universities in the form of Information Kinetics, Inc.'s, kiNexus National Candidate Database. Working with a base of 1,800 universities and colleges, kiNexus collects computer résumés and then makes them available via CD-ROM to employers in search of qualified job seekers. Because companies pay to subscribe to kiNexus, there is usually no charge to students and alumni, and only a small cost to those not affiliated with a member university. As with Operation Transition, job seekers are categorized by education, skills, job experience, and preferences. If you would like to use kiNexus to further the scope of your job search but find that your university is not a member (check with your school's career guidance office), you can get further information by calling kiNexus at (800) 828-0422.

From the employers' standpoint, kiNexus is a time-saving tool that gives them access to a plenitude of qualified candidates. It is also a cost-efficient alternative to shelling out the cash for on-campus recruiting efforts. The standardized résumé format allows for easy comparison of candidates.

From the job seeker's perspective, the high-tech approach to job hunting is not quite so promising. Even advocates of technology do not believe that this should be a job seeker's only tool. But computer-assisted job hunting does represent another means of getting one's name in the hat. And since the service is free to many college-age job seekers and recent grads, what do you have to lose?

SAM MARSHALL
2615 River Mountain Drive
Boulder, CO 80303
(303) WAN-TJOB

OBJECTIVE

Marketing position, with an emphasis in sales

EDUCATION

B.S., Business Administration, emphasis in marketing
University of Colorado
Graduation: May 1993   GPA: 3.2/4.0

PRIMARY EXPERIENCE

AT&T, Campus Sales Representative, September 1992–May 1993
- Sold AT&T long-distance services to students
- Set team sales goal and reached 105 percent

Baxter Minority Seminar, Counselor, June 1992
- One of seven counselors responsible for 30 high school students
- Identified and recruited appropriate business leaders as speakers

KBCO AM/FM, Public Relations/Promotions Intern, January 1991–May 1991
- Organized FCC-required Business Leaders' Ascertainment Survey
- Assisted in promotion of the Kinetics Race, which drew more than 25,000 participants

Romano's Restaurant, Management Assistant, August 1989–August 1992
- Trained new employees in all aspects of the restaurant business
- Invested with sole managerial responsibility on designated closing nights

ACTIVITIES

University of Colorado Marketing Association, April 1992–April 1993
- Developed care-package project that raised just under $3,000
- Designed advertising campaign that raised membership by 40 percent

Dean's Cabinet, Student Representative, September 1991–May 1993
- One of 15 students selected from among 2,600 to discuss student issues with the dean

Leadership Council, Service Award, Fall 1992
- Selected by business school leaders to receive this award for outstanding achievements in the community and CU Business School

Vice President, April 1991–April 1992
- Recruited top professional speakers, including executives from Procter & Gamble and Ball Packaging and Products Group, to educate members
- Devised an itinerary of activities to keep members actively involved

Leadership Council, Representative, October 1990–April 1991
- Published résumé book that raised $2,000 to help fund student activities

COMPUTER SKILLS

MS Word, WordPerfect, Lotus 1-2-3, MS Excel

John H. Rodriguez

561 Pershing Boulevard
St. Louis, Missouri 63130
(314) 999-8686

EDUCATION

1993   B.S., Applied Psychology
Washington University

CAREER-RELATED EXPERIENCE

Fall 1992– Research Assistant to Dr. Sarah Roberts, Professor of Clinical Psychology
Spring 1993 • Recruited and screened research candidates for behavioral eating disorder study, in
accordance with Dr. Roberts' specifications
• Maintained study files on research participants
• Assisted in the compilation of research findings

Fall 1992   Teaching Assistant, Cognition and Consciousness
• Led weekly discussion groups to facilitate undergraduate comprehension of class readings
• Acted as liaison between professor and undergraduates

Summer   Intern, Mission Psychological Services
1992   • Maintained correspondence files from foster parents and caseworkers
• Compiled profiles and charted progress of foster children
• Observed psychological therapy

Fall 1991   Teaching Assistant, Introduction to Psychology
• Assisted professor with preparation of class materials and grading
• Tutored undergraduates

Fall 1990– Intern, Lincoln High School
Spring 1991 • Assisted in psychological testing of students
• Observed psychological counseling

ADDITIONAL EXPERIENCE

Fall 1988– Office Assistant, St. Louis Chamber of Commerce
Summer 1990 • Maintained filing system
• Handled tourist information requests
• Assisted in preparation of mass mailings

SKILLS   Working knowledge of Filemaker Pro
Type 55 wpm
Fluent in Spanish

INTERESTS   Travel, yoga, rock climbing

57

PETER JACKSON

EDUCATION   B.S., Radio, Television, and Film, June 1993
Northwestern University, Evanston, IL

EXPERIENCE   **WLS–TV,** Chicago, IL
Production Intern, Fall 1992–Present
- Assisted in production of a telethon, specials, and three weekly shows in programming department of station owned and operated by ABC-TV
- Screened videotapes and researched programming material
- Maintained guest and audience relations
- Created proposal for production of documentary on Chicago housing
- Wrote voice-overs for on-air promotion of shows
- Accompanied Electronic Field Production crews taping on location
- Typed audio onto TelePrompTer; wrote out cue cards

JIM HENSON PRODUCTIONS, New York, NY
Public Relations Intern, Summer 1992
- Compiled and designed three monthly publicity packages
- Maintained files and scrapbooks of newspaper and magazine clippings
- Researched material for upcoming Muppet projects
- Systematized and updated archives

ACTIVITIES   **WNUR,** Spring 1990–Present
- On-air news reporter and editorialist

NORTHWESTERN STUDENT TELEVISION, Spring 1992
- Collaborated on writing comedy sketches for "Now We're Talking"

STUDIO 22, Fall 1992
- Director of "Varsity Cafe," an award-winning situation comedy

SKILLS
- Conducting primary and secondary research
- Writing, both nonfiction and fiction
- Proficient in WordPerfect and Microsoft Word
- Working knowledge of Japanese

520 OAK STREET, SEATTLE, WASHINGTON 98177 (206) GET-AJOB

Susan Smith

Merrimack College
Ash 547
East Hanover, MA 01845
508-333-5555

Permanent Address (as of 6/1/93):
30 Main Avenue
North Quincy, MA 01845
508-211-2121

STRENGTHS
Solid academic background with diverse work experience; strong communication and interpersonal skills; thorough and precise attention to detail; excellent analytical and organizational skills; highly motivated

LEADERSHIP
Who's Who Among American College Students; Coordinator of the 1993 Business Banquet and Leadership Development Conferences; Co-coordinator of Peace and Social Justice Week (1991 and 1992); Team Leader, M.O.R.E.

CO–OP EXPERIENCE
1/92–8/92
KODAK ELECTRONIC PRINTING SYSTEMS/BILLERICA, MA
International Support Coordinator: Communicated worldwide with Kodak employees; responded to international inquiries, including monitoring, directing, and implementing solutions; coordinated and sent bimonthly communication packages; maintained accurate international distribution lists

5/91–8/91
IBM/WALTHAM, MA
Consultant Relations Representative: Acted as liaison between IBM and the consultant community; researched and distributed information on IBM hardware, software, service offerings, and education; coordinated consultant teleconferences; maintained consultant database

1/90–5/90
9/90–12/90
PENNWELL PUBLISHING/WESTFORD, MA
Computer Graphics World and *Type World* magazines
Marketing Assistant: Designed, edited, and proofread research studies, promotional materials, cover letters, surveys, media kits, and press releases; assisted in handling trade show and seminar logistics; attended and staffed various trade shows; developed reprints for sale and coordinated the product, price, promotion, and distribution; telemarketed to service readers and to sell advertising space; interacted with ad agencies, printer, show managers, hotels, and travel agencies; created databases on Macintosh and IBM

ADDITIONAL EXPERIENCE
5/90–Present
MERRIMACK COLLEGE/NORTH ANDOVER, MA
Resident Assistant: Coordinate resident programs; develop a community environment; serve as resource person and peer counselor; uphold, enforce, and educate students about college rules, regulations, and policies

6/88–2/90
CVS/NORTH ANDOVER, MA
Shift Supervisor and District Trainer: Trained and supervised employees; resolved customer problems; balanced cash drawers; computed sales receipts; tallied and reported time cards; opened and closed store

EDUCATION
MERRIMACK COLLEGE
B.S., Business Administration, 1993; Major: Marketing; GPA in major: 3.4
Self-supported 85 percent of college tuition and expenses

COMPUTER SKILLS
MacWrite II, WriteNow, WordPerfect, Microsoft Word, PageMaker, Adobe Illustrator, QuarkXpress, MacDraw, Excel, Filemaker Pro, Print Shop, Pascal, SPSS

ACTIVITIES
American Marketing Association; Who's Who Among American College Students Selection Process Committee; Resident Assistant and Campus Ministry Search Committee; Orientation Committee

Mary Anne Lawrence

410 South Jackson Street
Austin, Texas 78701
(512) 222-6666

Permanent Address (as of 6/1/93):
53 Lakeside Drive
New York, New York 10023
(212) 999-6663

EDUCATION

University of Texas, Austin   B.A., Journalism, public relations concentration (1993)

PROFESSIONAL EXPERIENCE

Manning, Selvage & Lee
(New York, New York)

Public Relations Intern, Summer 1992
- Assisted account executives in consumer and travel divisions with research and program development for AmeriFlora '92, Norelco, and Polaroid

Hyde & Partners
(London, England)

Public Relations Intern, Spring 1991
- Assisted account supervisor with corporate accounts: Dow Europe, Incorporated Society of British Advertisers, Elizabeth Gage Jewelry Collection
- Created brochure for Audit Bureau of Circulations

Boston University
International Programme
(London, England)

Public Relations Intern, Spring 1991

Dorf & Stanton Communications
(New York, New York)

Public Relations Intern, Summer 1990
- Assisted account executives in organizing the Moosehead Beer "Share the Wilderness" campaign for Guinness Import Company

ACTIVITIES

Chief Articles Editor
Texas Journalism Review Vol. VIII (Fall 1992)
- Solicited, evaluated, and selected student submissions

Alumni Relations Chairperson
UT School of Communications (Fall 1992–Spring 1993)
- Organized annual fund-raising drive
- Created reunion brochures

COMPUTER SKILLS

Familiar with WordPerfect, MacWrite, QuarkXpress

INTERESTS

Art, fashion, theater, skiing, tennis, travel

The Cover Letter

Your cover letter is the personalizing factor in an otherwise impersonal document, your résumé. A successful cover letter highlights and enhances the information on your résumé, targeting it toward a specific prospective employer.

—Merrimack College

Unlike the résumé, which is primarily in bullet-point format, the cover letter is your chance to capture a prospective employer's interest by affording him or her a brief but informative glance at the personality—and the person—behind your résumé. In addition to providing you with a forum in which to demonstrate your ability to write clearly and concisely, the cover letter offers you three distinct opportunities to establish a link between yourself and your prospective employer:

1) You are able to highlight any benefits that you offer the employer, particularly those that may not be readily apparent from a swift glance at your résumé.

2) You have an opportunity to draw some parallels between your skills and the skills needed in the potential job, especially valuable to those people whose job histories are not obviously connected to the jobs they are seeking.

3) You may personalize the application process further by including additional information, such as why you are interested in this line of work and/or this particular company.

THE BASICS

- To get a prospective employer's attention, your cover letter must be personalized with names and references to the company. Never send a cover letter addressed "Dear sir or madam" or "To whom it may concern." When addressing a letter to a female recipient, you should also try to ascertain whether she uses "Miss," "Mrs.," or "Ms." When in doubt, go with "Ms." When responding to a "blind ad"—that is, a newspaper ad with a box number—you should use the salutation, "Dear prospective employer."
- Never, ever send a form cover letter. Sure, there are some aspects of each letter's content that may not change, such as how you initially became interested in a particular line of work, but overall, you should strive to personalize each letter as much as possible. Also, if you are using a word processor to create "new" letters via cut-and-paste, make certain that all "pastes" are free of references that are specific to other companies or other situations.
- As in the writing of your résumé, the importance of accuracy cannot be overstated. Take special care to spell the recipient's name correctly, to use his or her correct title, and to use the company's complete and correct address. If you have any doubts, check with the company's receptionist, switchboard operator, or human resources department to verify all necessary information.

61

- A cover letter's appearance must adhere to all the conventions of the résumé, including the same paper with the same font or type style and absence of errors. A block-style letter, in which all lines are flush with the left margin and a space is included between paragraphs, is the easiest to type, looks most professional, and is the most common style of business letter.

THE SPECIFICS

A cover letter should be no more than one page and, depending upon the format you use, will typically consist of three to five paragraphs, each with its own purpose. Once you have mastered the format, making modifications for different positions along the same career path is simple. Two basic outlines follow (sample letters 2 and 3 follow the same format but are for different types of positions):

Sample Cover Letter #1

Put your current address and phone number at the top right-hand corner of the page. (Your permanent address need appear on your résumé only.) Do not include your name at the top of the page, since that will be saved for the closing.

1500 South Utica
Tulsa, OK 74110
(918) 555-1034

Your letter should always be personalized to include the recipient's name, title, company, and address. The date should be below the recipient's address and to the right.

Ms. Michelle Roberts
Manager of Human Resources
National Corporation
5000 Skillman Road
Dallas, TX 24500

February 8, 1993

Dear Ms. Roberts,

Paragraph 1: Identify the position for which you are applying and note where you learned about the opening, whether it was from an ad, word-of-mouth, or your own personal research. If you were referred by a networking contact or company employee, always mention it.

I would like to apply for the MIS systems analyst position with National Corporation. Mr. Steve Crowley in your accounting department suggested that I forward my résumé to you. I believe the position would be a good fit with my skills and experience.

Paragraph 2: Relate your experience and skills to the qualifications needed for the desired position. If your experience is not in the same field, draw parallels and note similarities, or risk being eliminated. The skills and experience mentioned should be prominently listed on your résumé. Yes, this may entail tailoring your résumé to specific positions, but that's just one more reason to use a computer in the job-search process. Also, make reference to your enclosed résumé.

This position requires knowledge of networked microcomputer software applications, with an emphasis on DBase III and Lotus 1-2-3. I have majored in management information systems (MIS), with an emphasis on networked microcomputers, and have written programs for end users in DBase III and Lotus, in addition to being fluent in three programming languages. I understand your system utilizes both DOS and Windows, and I have experience in both operating systems. Practical experience gained as an end-user consultant at Eastern Oil during my internship has given me valuable insight into the day-to-day operation of an MIS department. I have enclosed my résumé, which furnishes you with additional information regarding my skills and qualifications.

Paragraph 3: Tell the reader why you are interested in this job, field, and/or company.

My experience and career goals appear to match this position very well. I am confident that I can perform the job effectively. Your company has an outstanding reputation, and Mr. Crowley recommends it highly to me. I am very much interested in the systems analyst position, and in working for National Corporation.

Paragraph 4: Ask for the interview and state a time when you will be calling to follow up. (Be sure to record this date in your daily planner, so you can make a positive impression by being punctual.)

Please consider my request for a personal interview to further discuss my qualifications and this job opportunity. I will call next week to see whether a meeting may be arranged. Please feel free to call me at (918) 555-1034 in the interim.

Paragraph 5: Thank the reader for his or her time, and close with a positive note about meeting with him or her soon.

Thank you for your consideration. I look forward to meeting with you soon.

Sincerely,

[Handwritten signature]
Barbara Dunne

enclosure

Sample Cover Letter #2

Sample Cover Letter #1 is very effective because the applicant was able to draw many parallels between herself and the position she sought. You may not always have that much to say about a particular position or company, however. In that case, you should draft a cover letter that includes the same basic information but is less detailed. The format (address placement, closing, etc.) is the same as in Letter #1, but the letter consists of only three paragraphs and more closely resembles the following:

Paragraph 1: *I am applying for the position of Customer Service Representative, which was advertised in the* Boston Globe *on December 1.*

or

I am seeking a career opportunity with your firm in the area of marketing. I am particularly interested in customer service and sales.

or

John Smith, vice president of marketing for the SAME Company, suggested I contact you. I am seeking a career opportunity in marketing and am particularly interested in customer service and sales.

Paragraph 2: *My qualifications for this position include a bachelor's degree in marketing and three years of experience in telemarketing and customer service. I am especially adept at handling customer problems, and I have assisted in the design and implementation of a sales and service system. My strengths include my communication abilities and interpersonal skills. I enjoy meeting and interacting with people. The enclosed résumé will give you a more complete idea of my background and qualifications.*

Paragraph 3: *Thank you for your time and consideration. I will be contacting you early next week to discuss this opportunity further. In the interim, please feel free to contact me at 555-3333.*

or

Thank you for your time and consideration. If you feel that my skills and experience may meet your organization's needs, please call me at 555-3333.

Sample Cover Letter #3

Paragraph 1: *I am applying for the position of assistant gallery manager, which was advertised in the* San Diego Union Tribune *on February 21.*

or

I am seeking a full-time position with a small art gallery that supports artists who work in a variety of media. I am particularly interested in managing all aspects of special exhibits, from artist recruitment to exhibit promotion to the show itself.

or

I am contacting you at the suggestion of Betty Tyler, an artist whose work has appeared in your gallery a number of times. I am interested in joining the staff of a small gallery that is committed to providing socially committed artists with a public forum in which to show their work, and Ms. Tyler advised me that yours is such a gallery.

Paragraph 2: *My qualifications for this position include a bachelor's degree in fine arts and serving as a student representative on the university's search committee for a new chairperson of the fine arts department. In addition, I served for two years as a member and for one year as chairperson of Dartmouth's student hospitality committee, which is responsible for ensuring that the needs of each visiting artist are met and for organizing show openings. My strengths include my communication abilities and interpersonal skills. I enjoy meeting and interacting with people. The enclosed résumé will give you a more complete idea of my background and qualifications.*

Paragraph 3: *Thank you for your time and consideration. I will be contacting you early next week to discuss this opportunity further. In the interim, please feel free to contact me at 555-7825.*

or

Thank you for your time and consideration. If you feel that my skills and experience are an appropriate fit with your gallery's needs at this time, please call me at 555-7825.

Hot Tip: Managing Your Job Search.

In managing your job search, you should keep a record of every letter or phone call you make. If you are in contact with several companies (or even various people within the same company), this method will help you remember each person with whom you spoke and the specifics of the conversation. We also suggest recording in a daily planner the dates you indicated you would be calling someone so you will be right on cue when your call is expected.

Some job candidates have found it useful to write all information related to the job search on index cards. As the interviewing process progresses, they then move the cards to the appropriate section of the job search file (networking, interviewing, follow-up, offer, rejection, etc.). This method will help you to keep track of where you are in the process.

The Artful Approach to Résumés and Cover Letters

Some prospective employees attempt to stand apart from the crowd by offering a unique résumé. But when a student decides to undertake an artful approach to employment, he or she faces the risk of being rejected because of inappropriate behavior. Use an unusually creative approach only if you are seeking employment in a highly stylized, risk-oriented, or creative field, or if you are applying to a firm that encourages individuality. It is up to you to strike the appropriate balance.

ACHIEVING SWEET SUCCESS: Achieving success through the creative approach requires that you step outside of the box far enough to get noticed while still displaying the requisite level of professionalism. Consider the experience of DeeDee, a Johnson & Wales alumna, who found herself soon to be unemployed after only nine months of professional employment. Her employer, a hotel, was "downsizing." She had met numerous rock stars and other performers while working at the hotel, and decided she would like to work for a record company.

Since this career field is progressive and daring, DeeDee decided to make her résumé look like a CD. Using a clear plastic CD case, DeeDee put a color photograph of herself and a couple of guitars on the front, included her résumé on the back, and placed a cover letter inside. She left her "CD" at Polygram Records in Boston during her lunch break.

By the time DeeDee returned to her office, Polygram had already called her. During her interview, DeeDee was told that the firm had no openings. However, Polygram was so impressed with her that a job was created for her; DeeDee is now director of promotions for Polygram Records in the Northeast.

Good Attempts: As in any job search, the right approach must meet the right opportunity. The following examples are classified as "good attempts" because, although their ideas were as creative as DeeDee's, the timing was off. Because achieving success through use of the artful approach is a combination of calculated risk-taking and following one's instincts, it is especially important to follow up with prospective employers when the artfully approached job search doesn't go your way. This will enable you to determine whether your approach, your level of experience, or your timing was off base. For example, one applicant for an internship with CNN sent to her prospective employer a box that, when opened, released balloons to which her application and résumé were attached. She didn't get the job and, because she didn't follow up, now doesn't know whether that decision was based on her credentials, her approach, or a combination of the two. We'll give you more specifics about the art of following up in chapter 7, but for now, consider some of these attention-getting approaches:

- Johnson & Wales graduate Paul applied for a position with a well-known automotive magazine. His four-color résumé featured the magazine's cover with the words "And now introducing Paul" emblazoned on it. His cover letter, résumé, and reference sheet appeared inside and were graphically similar to the magazine.

  Paul has not yet been hired by his favorite magazine, but they liked and remembered his résumé. As he gains more professional experience, he periodically sends them letters reminding them of his interest. It would not be surprising if Paul works for this publication someday.

- One student who applied to the Walt Disney Corporation screened a logo of Mickey Mouse onto the background of his résumé.

- A student interested in the fashion field used paper for her résumé that had a bit of texture and a background design that resembled cloth.

- Interested in desktop publishing, one student printed on the back of his résumé the names of the equipment, software, and type styles used. Although it appeared in small print, the information subtly informed the employer that this job candidate had the appropriate knowledge and skills for the job.

Chapter 5

Networking: Tapping into the Hidden Job Market

You must design a job-search strategy that utilizes every possible tool and exploits every opportunity.

—Northeastern State University, University Center Tulsa

We've all heard the story "Oh, I got my job through my mom's brother's girlfriend's aunt, who knew someone in the sales department who was friends with a guy in the hiring department." And how about that old complaint "Well, the only reason *he* got the job is because he knew someone in the company"? These scenarios are more likely than you might think. Knowing someone (who knows someone who knows someone who knows the right person) is often how initial contacts are made.

In fact, more than 75 percent of job openings today are never advertised because advertising to fill personnel needs is usually seen as a last resort. When a position needs to be filled, the most likely scenario goes something like this: Employers first think of likely candidates that they know. These might include people who already work for the company but in a different position, as well as people who have made their interest in the company known through résumés, cover letters, or even phone calls. If no one comes to mind, employers often seek recommendations from employees and business associates before turning to the personnel department. With this informal job-search system in place, most jobs are filled before the need to advertise arises. Your task, therefore, is to bypass much of the competition by accessing decision makers at some point between the time they decide to hire someone and the time they contact the personnel department; by doing so, you will have effectively tapped into the "hidden" job market.

Networking is defined as the process of discovering and utilizing connections between people. You've no doubt heard the term, and there's a good chance that society's tendency to equate *networking* with *schmoozing* has left you with a negative attitude toward the entire process. But before you allow negative press to dissuade you from making use of your most valuable key to the hidden job market, take another look at the ways in which networking can be beneficial not only to you, but to all of the people in your network.

The purpose of networking is 1) to gather information and advice regarding the industries or companies in which you are interested, 2) to receive help with fine-tuning your approach to the job search and your résumé, and 3) to obtain referrals to other professionals who can offer similar information. The ultimate goal, of course, is a job. Think of your network as people on the inside who can let you in the back door. At first you may feel as though you are using people to your own advantage, and to a certain extent, you are. What you should also realize, however, is that despite the so-called tough competition in the job market, it is still very difficult for an employer to find a candidate who he or she feels is perfect for the job. Networking benefits prospective employers because a personal reference gives them some added assurance.

Along the same lines, you should never allow yourself to feel guilty about utilizing a networking contact. No matter how influential your networking contacts are in helping you connect with the right people and opportunities, *you* have to get the job, and *you* have to keep it. Once that job is yours, don't let anyone take the wind out of your sails with such comments as "You knew someone, right?"

Networking Tips
- Never forget that *everyone you meet is a potential contact.*
- Be sure to *end every conversation by asking for a business card.* Keep them on file.
- *Never ask a contact for an internship, interview, or job.*
- One of the keys to successful networking is to get as many people involved in the process as possible. Your goal is to *make your career interests known to everyone,* from the president of your bank to your Uncle Joe.
- *Incorporate networking into your daily life.*
- *Always send a note of thanks* to any contact who has been particularly helpful.

why should I NETWORK?

- New information
- New ideas
- New friends
- New methods for doing things more creatively and more efficiently
- New leads

Networking motto: A friend of a FRIEND IS Your FRIEND

PROSPECTING: WHOM YOU KNOW AND HOW THEY CAN HELP
The first step in building your network is to generate a list of people you already know. Chances are, you already have the beginnings of a core network; it's just that you haven't necessarily thought of it as such. Begin by asking yourself the following questions (needless to say, you shouldn't put down everyone you know, just those people who might be able to assist you in your job search):

Whom do I know in my family?
Mother/father
In-laws
Brothers/sisters
Aunts/uncles
Other relatives

Whom do I know from among my past employers?
Former coworkers
Customers, clients
Former competitors
Former bosses

Whom do I know from my present employer?
Coworkers
Customers, clients
Competitors
Management

Whom do I know from my school days?
Professors
Administrators
Resident advisers
Members of student organizations
Sorority sisters/fraternity brothers
Classmates (and their parents)
Career counselors
Placement advisers
Alumni

Whom do I know from my hobbies?
Club members
Members of special interest groups
Sports team
Athletic club members
Aerobics class
Fellow volunteers

Whom do I know from my past?
Neighbors
Friends
Members of the armed forces

Which other professionals do I know?
Doctors
Politicians
Accountants
Lawyers
Bankers

Whom do my parents know?
Coworkers
Friends

Now that you've determined who your contacts are, it may be useful at this point to establish a network file. We recommend using index cards, on which you can record each person's name, address, and phone number, as well as such additional information as his or her hobbies, the kind of work he or she does, the groups to which he or she belongs, etc. These individualized index cards are also a good place to record telephone and in-person contact with your networkee.

Next, divide your prospect list into four nonexclusive categories:
1) Influential people in your field of interest who have the authority to hire
2) People who might have leads on jobs
3) People who might be willing to refer you to others
4) People who have contacts in a particular area of the country (or world) in which you would like to work

With your lists in order, consider yourself off to a good start. Keep reading to determine how all those names and numbers can best be utilized in your job search.

Networking: Establishing Contacts on an Ongoing Basis

Although networks naturally form with our friendships and business relationships, the art of networking involves actively seeking out new friends and business contacts as well. Anyplace where people gather should be recognized as an opportunity to establish new contacts.

SYSTEMATIC NETWORKING

To expand your network systematically, you will be taking two basic approaches: referrals and "cold calling."

Students who are new to the networking ritual may initially be more comfortable using the referral approach. This approach entails building a bridge from a person whom you know, to a person who may be able to help you or even lead you to a job.

Let's say, for example, that you know a Ms. Jones, a friend of the family, who manages the advertising budget for your local food mart. While talking to her, you discover that her company does its advertising through Boston-based Gulko Advertising, which happens to be the advertising agency for which you'd most like to work. You do not want a job from Ms. Jones; you simply want information she might have. So you ask Ms. Jones whether she would be willing to set up a meeting between you and her contact at Gulko. This situation is much better than walking into the agency and asking to talk to someone in personnel.

From the prospect lists you developed, choose the people you feel will be of most help to you and contact them for an informational interview. An informational interview, which will be discussed in more detail later in this chapter, is an arranged meeting between you and a person whose professional accomplishments and/or industry are of interest to you. Once you have contacted everyone on your "first choice" list, go back to your list of untapped contacts and choose another group of names. If you network effectively, you'll notice that your list of untapped contacts will grow rather than shrink. This is because each person you meet in a networking situation is a potential source of additional contacts.

If you consider yourself confident and assertive, you might want to try your hand at cold calling. As the name implies, you are calling someone whom you would like to know, but who has no idea who you are. While some people find this approach intimidating, it is often the only way to gain access to potential contacts with whom you are not able to establish a referral bridge. To be successful using this approach, you must be persistent (but never obnoxious or irritating), and remember not to take rejections personally. As with selling, networking is a numbers game grounded in the principles of probability, and every 25 no's will probably yield at least one yes.

OPPORTUNISTIC NETWORKING

Small talk can turn into important talk at the blink of an eye.
—Missouri Western State College

Everyone you meet is a potential contact. Even the briefest encounter with a person sitting next to you on an airplane, standing in line with you at the movies, or giving a guest lecture to your ethics class should not be ruled out. For example, while attending an American Marketing Association conference, a New Mexico State University student was lucky enough to find himself at a seminar hosted by a top executive of an airline company. Following the seminar, the student took the opportunity to thank the gentleman for his words of inspiration. He also expressed his interest in working for an airline. Before leaving, the soon-to-be graduate picked up a business card for his network file. When the time came to draw upon his job-search resources, the card proved to be his most valuable tool. When contacting the speaker several months later, the student was pleasantly surprised to find that the gentleman remembered him vividly. This initial contact eventually led to a job in the airline industry.

It is important to realize that *you can create your own opportunities by being in the right place at the right time*. The following is a list of some recommended "right places":
- Career services volunteer groups. Volunteers have an advantage because of the contacts they make through these groups. It gives them a chance to meet with employers in an informational, nonpressure situation.
- Chamber of commerce functions in your area, as well as in the cities in which you hope to be employed. You can introduce yourself to professionals and discuss opportunities available to you.
- Informational meetings given by companies. Sometimes these are held on campus; other times they're held at the company itself.
- Trade shows. There are trade shows for just about every industry, and there is bound to be one related to your interests. Contact a professional organization in your field of choice and find out when and where the trade shows will be held. You don't have to be an employed professional to attend; you just have to register. Once there, meet as many people as you can. At the very least, be sure to pick up available business cards (valuable for obtaining names) and company brochures.

Hot Tip: In opportunistic networking, personal networking cards are of particular importance, because these networking encounters may be very brief. Exchanging cards is a 10-second process that creates a link between you and your

73

potential contact. From a practical standpoint, if you don't know where a person works and are unable to remember his or her name, you haven't made a contact. Networking cards, containing the information below, look like traditional business cards and are for people conducting a job search:

Anita Job
B.S., Finance
New Mexico State University
Class of 1994

	Permanent Address (as of 6/94):
007 Spruce Lane	662 Champion Way
Las Cruces, New Mexico 88007	Birmingham, Alabama 35201
(505) 555-3241	(205) 555-6982

The personal networking card allows you to distribute your name and number to virtually anyone—regardless of the availability of pen and paper. It also allows potential employers to identify your face with a name and phone number. Most quick-print shops will design and print networking cards for around $30 per hundred. Don't forget to check with your campus career center to determine whether your university has arranged for a student discount at one of the local print shops.

Informational Interviews

The short-term goal of networking is an informational interview. Whether your contact is a new acquaintance met at a local pub or a long-time friend of your grandmother, your first objective is to arrange a meeting that will afford you the opportunity to acquire key information, advice, and additional referrals. Ideally, these meetings are in person, because it helps when a contact is able to connect a name to a face. When a particular contact has limited time, however, you may want to arrange for a telephone interview. The advantage of getting your feet wet through informational interviews with people you already know (even remotely) is that the process is less intimidating. Remember: all you are asking from them is advice and assistance; most people who have the time will gladly give it. When calling to ask if you can set up an appointment, first ask whether the person has a few minutes to talk. Not everyone will have the time, but don't be discouraged. Simply ask when it would be convenient for you to call back. For the hard-to-reach contact, take advantage of unexpected opportunities (or create your own opportunities) by speaking to them at meetings or functions.

Once you've landed an informational interview, there are a few simple rules to follow. Perhaps most important: **Do not walk in with a "What can you do for me?" attitude**. Although both you and your contact know that you are seeking information about the company and/or industry, it is important to realize that your interviewer is doing you a favor by taking time out of his or her workday to answer your questions.

Unlike most interview situations you will encounter in your job search, the informational interview is your opportunity to ask questions. As a result, the usefulness of an informational interview depends almost entirely on your efforts. The best way to prepare for an informational interview is to **conduct preliminary research about the company and industry**. This will enable you to ask informed, pertinent questions. Although your stated and primary objective is to gain insight and information from the contact about the company/industry, your secondary objective is to leave him or her with a clear impression of how your interest and skills can benefit a potential employer. Your level of preparedness for the interview will be one of the indicators by which the person judges your professionalism and interest.

While conducting your discussion, **make it a point to use open-ended questions**. This is very important, because you don't want the person to yes-and-no you to death. You want to elicit useful, in-depth information. The only way this will happen is if you ask such well-thought-out questions as "Could you tell me a little bit more about the challenges you are currently facing in your company/industry?" For additional suggestions, consult the "Asking a Few Questions of Your Own" section in chapter 6.

You may ask an informational interviewee almost any work-related question, including questions related to his or her personal career goals and experiences. Under no circumstances, however, should you ask for a job. This is an informational interview, and you don't want to place your contact in a potentially awkward situation. Instead, **let your contact know you are considering job possibilities and seeking information**. Explain your situation frankly, and then ask for a job referral to aid your job hunt. This will focus your conversation on your achievements and elicit camaraderie, and should also result in your contact genuinely wanting to help you.

In all conversations related to your employment goals, it is best to **be as specific as possible about your talents and what kind of position you are looking for**. Being specific ensures that your name and the position you seek will stay on your contact's mind when he or she hears information that may be of help to you.

As you become more experienced in informational interviews (or any other interview, for that matter), you will no doubt discover that you may not like or agree with everyone you meet. When this is the case, it may help to remember that even an unpleasant experience could be the link to your dream job. You should **always be polite**. A little respect will go a long way toward achieving your informational goals.

Finally, don't forget to **say thank you**. As with any stage in your job search, it is important to express your appreciation to those who have helped you. By letting your contact know how his or her suggestions and referrals have worked for you, you are telling that person that you wish to maintain an ongoing relationship. The best way to do this is with a phone call or, preferably, a thank-you letter. For sample thank-you letters, refer to chapter 7.

Developing References

It is important to realize that the end of an informational interview should mark the beginning of a long-term relationship. Although networking contacts initially serve primarily as sources of information, these relationships, when nurtured, can be even more valuable as you progress in your career. Your relationship with each contact will be different depending upon the degree to which he or she is willing and able to help develop the personal chemistry between the two of you. Regardless, you should never lose complete touch with a contact you consider useful. We don't mean to imply that you should call each of your contacts every week—or every month, for that matter—but you should develop a list of "key" contacts with whom you want to communicate on a regular basis. This list should be a combination of those people who have expressed the most enthusiasm for helping you with your search, and those people whom you deem most useful. While communication with key contacts will be more frequent during your job search, even after you've found a position, you should initiate some form of communication with every contact at least once every six months.

Calling a contact just to say hello is OK, but sometimes that routine gets a little tiring. Remember to keep in touch in creative as well as traditional ways with those you meet:

- If you know of a particular outside interest of your contact, refer to it in your written and verbal exchanges, mentioning or even enclosing (for example) recent articles, announcements, etc.
- Keep your contacts abreast of your plans by sending them copies of your current résumé.
- Be sure to send out any news of your career-related achievements and awards.
- Invite your contacts to any professional activities you have helped to organize or panel discussions in which you are involved.

When you feel that a particular networking contact knows you well enough for you to speak comfortably (and positively) about your accomplishments, ask permission to use the person as a professional reference. For information on developing a reference sheet, see the "References" section of chapter 4.

When Should I Stop Networking?

The short answer is "Never," because networking is a continuous process. Although you may think a job offer signals the end of your networking, it's really just the beginning. Networking is a lifelong process. If anything, networking will come more easily once you are an industry "insider." The more relationships you are able to forge within your industry, the better.

Even after you have accepted a job, network contacts can be valuable sources of information and advice to you. Keeping your network file up-to-date ensures that you have an easy reference guide of contacts whenever you need assistance.

It is important to realize, too, that no matter how hard you work, how well you perform, or how necessary your product or service is in today's environment, you may once again find yourself in the job market. If this happens, your business relationships will open doors for you.

On a more positive note, you should also remember that one day *you* may be the person who is searching for that perfect job candidate. Having a strong network in your industry will better enable you to fill the position efficiently and effectively.

Chapter 6

The Interview

You have astounded your dream company with your networking skills and your strong résumé. Your reward? The much-coveted interview. At last, you've got your foot in the door. Suddenly, you envision what this means: a recruiter sitting across a large desk, drilling you with virtually unanswerable questions, one right after another. A bead of sweat forms on your brow, and you imagine the recruiter ripping apart your résumé, your accomplishments, and your pride. Soon you've convinced yourself that you might not want that interview at all.

STOP! Relax. With adequate preparation, the interview process doesn't have to be nearly *that* bad. Not all job interviews are conducted by company recruiters, so one of the first things to realize is that the interviewer may be just as unfamiliar with the process as you are. On the other hand, certain companies are known for their tough recruiters. Knowing what to expect during an interview—and how to react appropriately—will enable you to meet all types of interviewers with confidence.

What Is an Interview All About?

The first step in preparing for an interview is understanding the company's purpose for meeting with you. There are many reasons why a company likes to meet face-to-face with its applicants:

- Regardless of the position for which one is applying, companies today are looking for people who can *communicate*. An interview is the perfect opportunity for the employer to find out just how well you can do that, as well as to judge your interpersonal skills.
- The employer is also trying to find out exactly how you think, both critically and analytically. That's why so many interviewers ask questions that require you to demonstrate your thinking and problem-solving abilities. ("How would you teach a blind elephant not to cross the street against the light?" or "How many times does the average person say *the* in a given day?" or "How many gas stations are there in America?") Interviewers who ask these types of questions aren't expecting you to pull the "right" answer out of your hat; they simply want to determine whether your thought processes are logistically sound.
- A company also wants to know how knowledgeable and experienced you really are. Résumés are notorious for being, shall we say, a touch overstated? The interview allows the employer to probe for details.
- The interview is also a prospective employer's (and prospective employee's) opportunity to make sure that the "personality" of the company and that of the individual are compatible. If the company has a conservative, blue-suit, bottom-line personality, and the interviewee is a casual, I'll-get-it-done-when-I-can kind of person, the company and/or the individual might have incompatible expectations and performance standards. Don't forget to look upon the interview process as your chance to take measure of the company as well.
- Lastly, the interviewer wants to make sure that the candidate has an interest in the job. If you truly want the job, an interviewer should be able to sense your enthusiasm.

Most certainly, this list is not all-inclusive. And depending on the interviewing company's policies and corporate culture, some of these factors may be weighted more heavily than others. The key thing to remember is that the interviewer wants to find out about *you*. And don't forget, the interviewer is also evaluating many other applicants for the same position. Your responsibility is to make sure you are one of the candidates who stand out in that person's mind after a long day of interviews.

INTERVIEW TYPES

In its simplest form, an interview is an exchange of information between an employer and prospective employee. It is a conversation intended to help both parties learn as much as possible about each other within a limited time. Before preparing for the interview, however, it is helpful to be aware of the various types of interviews in which you may be invited to participate.

- **The Screening Interview:** The screening interview aims to assess the skills and personality traits of the potential candidate. The intent is to determine whether those skills and traits meet the criteria for the position in question. It is a broad-based meeting, generally conducted by the personnel department. The objective is to "screen out" those applicants the interviewer feels should not be hired, and "screen in" those who are judged appropriate to move on to the next level of interview. *Your* purpose is to convince the interviewer that you make the grade.

- **The General/Structured Interview:** The next step is often the general or structured interview, although in the interest of time, this interview may be combined with the screening interview. Typically conducted by a supervisory manager, the general interview is a one-to-one discussion that aims to determine whether your being hired is in the best interest of both parties. Be prepared for this one because you will be talking about specifics of the position, company, and industry.

- **The Social Interview:** The social interview can take place in a variety of nontraditional settings (lunch, cocktail party, plant/office tour, career day,etc.). More often than not, it will not resemble an interview in the traditional sense. It generally provides the employer with a good indication of how you might fit into the organization. The atmosphere may be highly informal, but do not let your guard down. Although you may not be asked questions directly related to your qualifications, continue to make positive statements that stress your experience and skills throughout the conversation. Make sure you don't overdo it, though; the interviewer will also want to know that you have social skills. (Appropriate: Interviewer—"This is a very good caterer." You—"Yes. I helped to manage a catering operation while I was in high school. It's a demanding job." Inappropriate: Interviewer—"Try this cheesecake, it's delicious." You—"Did I mention that I'm fluent in COBOL?")

Hot Tip: When meeting a prospective employer in a social setting for dinner, it is recommended that you eat something before you go. "What? Give up a free meal?" Yes. If your mind is on your stomach, you won't be as alert when answering questions. Also—no matter how tempted you may be—it's a good idea to avoid drinking or smoking until after you've been offered the job. People who drink or smoke generally understand why others choose not to indulge; people who abstain can be less tolerant.

- **The Sequential Interview:** Some companies use a series of interviews to evaluate candidates. Interviewers may include several supervisors, managers, and/or peers. Each person may cover the same material, or each may focus on a particular aspect of your qualifications. In either case, treat each interview as the first, and be sure to mention all your relevant qualifications to each person.

- **The Group Interview:** This is an interview that involves little old you and two or more interviewers. This technique is often used to make a more efficient use of interviewing time and to determine your ability to work cohesively within a group (not to mention your ability to withstand intense pressure). Each person in the group will ask questions, and they will all evaluate your responses. One suggestion is to answer each question while looking at the person who asked it, then follow with a short summary sentence directed to the group leader.

- **The Stress Interview:** As competition in the job market becomes more aggressive, it is conceivable that the frequency of stress interviews will surge, particularly for positions that require candidates to cope with a great deal of pressure. During the interview, an attempt will be made to unnerve you. For example, you may be constantly and deliberately interrupted; your answers may be met with nothing more than a cold, emotionless stare; or questions may be fired off at you in relentless, rapid-fire succession. Your objective: remain calm, continue to focus on communicating your strong points, and ride out the interview. Remember, the interviewer's main concern is to find out how you will react under pressure. Be a professional!

- **The Confrontational Interview:** A press relations professional reported that at an interview conducted after her graduation, she was taken aback by the question "What do you think of the gun control issue?" This is actually part of a technique known as the "confrontational" interview. In this type of interview, seemingly unrelated and often emotionally charged questions are asked in order to gauge whether an applicant is informed (remember what we said about reading the paper?) and can work effectively under pressure. The professional stumbled through the answer well enough to get the job, and after several years of working with journalists, she now realizes that the question was posed to her because it mirrors the job of a press relations expert.

What *should* one do in these situations? The important thing to remember is to think before you speak. You basically have four options: 1) tell the truth, with the knowledge that your answer may be at odds with that of the interviewer; 2) refuse to answer the question, with the knowledge that your interviewer may interpret this as a hostile response; 3) explain that you haven't had the opportunity to explore the situation fully, and therefore can't make an informed opinion; or 4) remain neutral by making a statement such as "Gun control is a complicated issue, and I can see both sides. Because incidents with handguns result in such a high number of deaths, both intentional and accidental, my natural inclination is to support gun control. By the same token, I understand that people who live in a violent society are concerned with self-protection and want to protect their right to bear arms. What is your opinion?"

How Do I Prepare for an Interview?

There are three phases of interview preparation: **researching the company, learning to answer questions,** and **learning to ask questions.** Don't underestimate the importance of any of these three phases, and don't make the mistake of going into an interview expecting to "wing it." The interview process is a competition. Receiving a job offer is dependent upon a combination of being better prepared and better qualified than the other candidates. Two weeks before an interview, there is probably not much you can do to enhance your résumé. But practice will always increase the skill with which you answer—and ask—questions during an interview, and every hour spent familiarizing yourself with a company will pay off during the interview.

RESEARCHING THE COMPANY

FACT: *Northwestern University asked 500 employers which job applicants' behaviors, responses, or activities were negative or counterproductive. The most popular responses to this question were: being unprepared for the interview, and not knowing much about the company or industry.*

—Missouri Western State College

The interview process starts long before you actually meet an interviewer. First, you must thoroughly research the employer. This will impress the person with whom you meet because it demonstrates that you have taken an interest in the organization and are likely to be enthusiastic about working there. Because the interviewer does not have to spend too much time describing the company and its background, you and the interviewer will have more time to discuss aspects of the position and the company that are not available through secondary sources; you will also have added time to convince the interviewer that you are the right person for the job. In addition, knowing such information as the size of the organization, the location of the facilities, its major competitors and clients, products or services offered, training provisions, relocation policies, and organizational structure will better enable you to determine whether the organization fits your needs and wants.

It would also be helpful to research trends, issues, and problems facing the organization in particular and the industry as a whole. Keep notes on such important facts as recent mergers, acquisitions, and stock splits. That information, as well as the organization's annual report, can give you a fairly decent picture of a company's/industry's financial condition. In the process of researching, be sure to jot down any relevant questions you may later have for the interviewer.

Ideally, you will have a head start on this research, based on your preliminary investigation into the company before you decided to submit your résumé; but if you never quite got around to it, *now* is the time to get started. First, refer back to the "Company by Company" section of chapter 2 for specific suggestions on topics that you should check into. Information is available through career placement offices, libraries, professional associations, computer databases, books, journals, directories, magazines, and newspapers. You may also call or write to the organization with which you will be interviewing to ask for such corporate material as annual reports and informational brochures.

Talking with informed people is another excellent way to get information about a company and its corporate culture that you won't find in its annual report. Let it be known that you are interested in a particular organization, and see whether any of your networking contacts have information that might prove helpful to you. A word of caution, however: all verbal information—both positive and negative—should be considered biased material; be wary of rumors.

If possible, establish a contact that will allow you to personally assess the corporate culture. Make contact with an individual within the company who is currently employed in a position similar to the one you are seeking. Ask this person to allow you to "shadow" him or her during a workday, so that you can gain valuable insight into the position. When seeking his first job, one New Mexico State University student did exactly that. By making a few phone calls before his first interview with a pharmaceutical company, he found a contact willing to be observed for a day. He recalls that this action gave him two advantages: 1) it showed his future employer that he was genuinely interested in the company, and 2) it confirmed his own interest to himself.

An often-overlooked part of preinterview research is an actual visit to the location where the interview will take place. Pay close attention to how you will get there on the day of the interview. If you are using public transportation, be sure to allow plenty of time. If you are driving, map out in advance how to get there, and be sure to check out the parking situation. Many of us take such things for granted, but not taking these steps can result in a stress-filled commute to the interview or, even worse, tardiness. Rarely is there an adequate excuse for being late to an interview.

Hot Tip: When researching a company, be sure to take note of key officers' names. If your interviewer mentions the president of the company by name only, and you greet the name with a blank stare, there may be some doubt as to how much you really know (and really want to know) about the company.

LEARNING TO ANSWER QUESTIONS AND COMMUNICATE EFFECTIVELY

Every interviewer has a different style of interviewing. For this reason, you shouldn't try to memorize the questions or your answers. Preparing for common categories of questions, however, will help to ensure that you are not caught off guard when a particular question is asked. Having a general idea of the points you are trying to convey will not only help you to give a complete, structured answer, but will also allow you to appear spontaneous in your response. Your goal is to leave the interviewer with the impression that you were prepared but natural.

Because the interviewer's purpose is to find out more about you, **open-ended questions** are commonly used in interviews. An open-ended question is one that invites a broad, detailed response. An example might be "Tell me a little about your experience as a youth counselor."

A **closed question** asks for specific data (usually a short answer). As the interviewee, you might want to turn a closed question into an open one, so that more information can be shared. For example, in response to the question "Do you have any sales experience?" you might reply: "I developed my selling skills as a member of the corporate sponsorship committee of the University of Colorado Psychology Association. In this position, I called on corporations in the UC community to convince them that a donation to our chapter could be beneficial to them in many ways, including advertising in our newsletter, word-of-mouth publicity from our members on campus, and of course, a tax deduction. It was definitely a learning experience, and I look forward to further using and developing my skills in an actual sales representative position."

It may be helpful to think of the interview questions as following a continuum, which serves as an excellent frame when preparing for your interview:

Past————————————————Present————————————————Future

Past

In past-oriented questions, the interviewer is looking for examples of prior accomplishments that could prove that you would be a good employee in the future. A popular (and sometimes dreaded) past-oriented question is "Tell me a little about yourself." Quite often, the interviewee takes this as a cue to recite his or her entire résumé. While this tactic does permit you to elaborate on your accomplishments, it also repeats everything the interviewer has already read about you. To attract the interest of the interviewer, divert the conversation away from your résumé by relating anecdotes about specific situations or accomplishments. For example, you could explain your motivation for attending your university or college, or how you happened to choose your major. These items are certainly not listed on your résumé, but they do help the interviewer learn a bit about how you think.

When describing your past accomplishments or experience, it is important to emphasize the ways in which you are different from other candidates. You should try to show how you have gone beyond the call of duty or used opportunity to your advantage. For example, many job candidates wait tables in restaurants as a means of supporting themselves through college. What distinguishes Amber, however, is that she became a wait-staff trainer and developed a uniform training program which included workshops and on-the-job training in order to create more consistency in the restaurant. That set Amber a step above all the other candidates, and chances are the recruiter will remember the interview.

Sometimes you will be given a negatively framed question. For example: "What was the most difficult problem you dealt with in your sales internship?" Simply listing an unsolved problem is sure to leave your recruiter unimpressed; instead, give a positive response to a negative question, thereby creating an opportunity to showcase your problem-solving skills. We recommend a three-step process that will allow the recruiter to "walk through" the situation with you: 1) state the problem clearly, 2) explain the actions you took to resolve the problem, and 3) describe the results of your actions. A well-thought-out answer to the above question might be the following:

"To prevent us from overlapping in our sales efforts, every representative was assigned a predetermined territory at the beginning of the summer. Unfortunately, the territories were established by someone who had never actually been to Wichita. I ended up with a territory that was the same size geographically as those of my colleagues, but because it was near the outskirts of the city, it was home to fewer businesses. At first this made me nervous, because I worried that I would be at a disadvantage when it came time to meet sales quotas. I knew that my selling technique would have to be different from that of other representatives, who spent their days visiting as many businesses as they could. I opted to spend more time with each business I called on, which meant that I had the time and opportunity to learn more about my customers and gain their trust. As it turned out, I was the number one representative by the end of the summer."

Remember: Emphasize what makes you different from all the other candidates. You want the recruiter to remember *you*.

Present

Present-oriented questions help the recruiter to determine why you might (or might not) be an excellent candidate for the position. Common present-oriented questions include "What can you offer this company?" and "Why should we hire you?" In this situation, it is tempting to simply list a number of adjectives that describe yourself (e.g.,"I'm a motivated, energetic, organized, strategic-thinking kind of person, who communicates his ideas well . . . "). At this point, the recruiter is most likely thinking, *Prove it*. And that is exactly what you must do. It is a good idea to group three to five of your strengths with examples that illustrate each strength. If, for example, you feel that one of your strengths is organization, you might "prove it" to an interviewer by using an example such as the following:

"I am a very organized person. As you can see from my résumé, I stay very busy. I'm a full-time student and a staff writer for the university paper, and I also work 30 hours each week as a waitress. In order to accomplish everything that must get done, I write all my tasks in my daily organizer, prioritize them, and plan my days accordingly. I have found that much more can be accomplished in this way."

Interviewers may also ask you to cite weaknesses. Job candidates often attempt to make up or list weaknesses that aren't weaknesses at all, a popular one being perfectionism. Employers have heard this one repeatedly—and, in most cases, would love to have a perfectionist working for them. But it's time we give recruiters a little credit; they see right through this canned answer and, for the most part, will be annoyed rather than impressed.

You can show honesty and maturity by admitting your real weaknesses. But as with negatively framed questions, you don't want to list a weakness and leave it "as is" for the interviewer to mull over at his or her convenience. Instead, show what you have done to convert that weakness into a strength. If you are a nervous public speaker, for example, explain that you have taken a class or joined a speech club in order to overcome your fear. It's best to avoid citing more than one or two weaknesses; you want to demonstrate your honesty, not massacre yourself!

Interviewers also use present-oriented questions to gauge your real interest in the company or industry. They may ask, "What do you know about our company?" If you've really done your homework, this question is a great opportunity for you to show that you have in-depth knowledge of the company. If you haven't done any research, however, this question can be a living hell! Blowing this question is a sure sign to the interviewer that you're unprepared, unknowledgeable, and downright uninterested in the company—none of which is likely to impress. Do your homework; there's no reason to drop the ball on this play.

No matter how much you think you know about the situation of a particular company, however, you never want to leave the interviewer with the impression that you think you know everything. Regardless of how many annual reports, magazine articles, newspaper features, or tabloid exposés are under your belt, you are still the outsider. Speak freely about what you know, but acknowledge that it is secondary information. If there is an issue related to your research that you wish to know more about, now is the time to ask. For example, "I read that new environmental controls are going to impact this industry heavily. What plans does the company have for complying with the new regulations?"

Future

Not surprisingly, interviewers use future-oriented questions to find out what your goals are. Perhaps the most common question is "What do you want to be doing in five years?" It is essential to have your homework done before these questions arise. Otherwise, you run the risk of naming goals that are incompatible with the company structure. For instance, mentioning a desire to move to the human resources department after working in marketing for a couple of years wouldn't make sense if the company does not hire human resources personnel from any other department. (Oops.) Such an answer not only makes you look unprepared, but also signals to the interviewer that his or her company cannot satisfy your career goals. It would be very risky for the company to hire you, therefore, because a lot of money and time would go into your training. If you won't be happy because you're not reaching your career goals, you are likely to leave the company or, at the very least, be dissatisfied and potentially unproductive in your work. You can avoid this situation by researching a company *before you apply*.

Practice Makes Perfect or, at the Very Least, Prepared

We recommend that in order to practice for an interview, you participate in mock interviews with guidance counselors at your career center as well as with friends or relatives. By participating in this process as early as your freshman or sophomore year, you will be better prepared for interviews both during and after college. In a mock interview, you have the opportunity to refine your answers to frequently asked questions. By reviewing your past accomplishments and successes in this manner, you can best decide how to work them into the conversation during an actual interview. You can *never* practice too much.

You should accept all interviewing opportunities that come your way. Even if you've decided that a particular company is not for you, participating in the interview process will offer you a chance to hone your skills and make a networking contact in your intended line of work.

50 Questions a Prospective Employer May Ask during an Interview

1. Tell me about yourself.
2. How would you describe yourself?
3. How would a close friend describe you?
4. Are you creative?
5. What do you consider to be your major strengths?
6. What do you consider to be your major weaknesses?
7. What is the most difficult work-related situation you have ever faced? How did you react?

(continued)

8. What two or three accomplishments have given you the most satisfaction? Why?
9. Can you give me an example of a time when you took the initiative at work?
10. Think of a crisis situation, during which things got out of control. Why did it happen, and what role did you play?
11. If you had your life to live over again, what would you do differently?
12. What are your short- and long-term goals? When and why did you establish these goals, and how are you preparing yourself to attain them?
13. What was your most rewarding college experience?
14. Why did you choose the career for which you are preparing?
15. Why did you select your college or university?
16. What college subjects did you enjoy the most? The least? Why?
17. Do you think your grades are a good indicator of your college achievement?
18. Do you plan to continue your education?
19. What extracurricular activities did you pursue?
20. Did you hold positions of leadership in any organizations?
21. What have you learned from your participation in extracurricular activities?
22. How has your college experience prepared you for a professional career?
23. If you had the chance to repeat your college career, what would you do differently?
24. Of the jobs that you have held, which did you enjoy the most/least? Why?
25. How would you describe the ideal job for you following graduation?
26. Why should I hire you?
27. Why did you seek a job with this company?
28. What criteria are you using to evaluate the company for which you hope to work?
29. What do you know about our company?
30. If you were hiring a graduate for this position, what qualities would you look for?
31. What do you think determines an individual's progress within a company?
32. What qualities do you prefer in a boss?
33. Can you give me an example of when you have "gone the extra mile"?
34. What relationship should exist between a supervisor and those reporting to him or her?
35. In what kind of work environment are you most comfortable?
36. What kinds of rewards are most satisfying to you?
37. How do these rewards affect the effort you put into your work?
38. How important is communication and interaction with others on the job?
39. What is your typical role as a group member?
40. Do you have a geographical preference?
41. Are you willing to relocate?
42. How do you feel about working overtime?

(continued)

43. What is your attitude toward overnight travel?
44. How would working evenings affect you?
45. Are you willing to spend at least six months as a trainee?
46. What kind of salary do you expect in five years?
47. What position do you expect to hold in five years? Ten years?
48. What can you do for us that someone else cannot do?
49. What special character traits of yours should I take into consideration?
50. How long will it take you to make a contribution to the company?

Five Tips on How to Answer These Questions Effectively

1. Before answering, determine what information the interviewer is trying to obtain. If the question is unclear, ask the interviewer to rephrase or clarify it.
2. Convey your strengths.
3. Relate your work experience, training, and personal strengths to the position for which you are interviewing.
4. Anticipate negative reactions, and practice how you will respond.
5. Stress what you can bring to the position/company.

Questions a Prospective Employer Cannot Ask

To prevent discrimination, national and state laws expressly prohibit employers from asking certain questions either on an application form or in a personal interview prior to selecting an employee. The specifics vary from state to state, but national guidelines exist. As stated in the Bureau of National Affairs' *Personnel Policy and Practice Series (April 1992)*:

Under federal and state equal employment opportunity laws, it is unlawful to discriminate on the basis of an applicant's race or ethnic group, national origin or citizenship, religion, sex, age, marital status, or disability. Therefore, raising a topic or asking a question pertaining to any of these protected subjects could be considered discriminatory, if the effect of the preemployment inquiry is to put the applicant at an employment disadvantage ("adverse impact") and the employer cannot show that the inquiry is related to a bonafide job requirement.

Interviewers can run into legal problems if they

- Solicit, directly or indirectly, information on social organizations or clubs to which the applicant belongs that indicate the race or color, national or ethnic origin, or religion of the membership.
- Inquire about the applicant's feelings toward working with coworkers of different races.
- Ask an applicant to specify where he or she, or parents or spouse, was born.

- Ask for a maiden name.
- Question applicants on their marital status, number and age of children, pregnancy, or future childbearing plans.
- Rate a candidate on English-language proficiency when such a skill is not a job requirement.
- Ask the applicant to describe a particular physical condition or disability, or to state whether he or she has ever been treated for specific diseases or medical conditions. It is also unlawful to ask applicants if they have ever been hospitalized and, if so, for what condition; if they have ever been treated by a psychologist; if they have had a major illness in the last five years; how many days they were absent from work in the last year due to illness; if they have any physical defects that would preclude them from performing certain kinds of work; if they are taking any prescribed drugs; if they have ever been treated for drug addiction or alcoholism; and if they have ever filed for workers' compensation insurance.
- Query the applicant on the type or condition of the applicant's discharge from military service.
- Inquire about arrest or conviction records.

Employers are advised to review all interview questions to determine how the answers to certain questions are used in making selection decisions. If responses appear to disqualify (or in fact do disqualify) from consideration for employment, a disproportionate number of the members of one group (e.g., minorities, women), the questions should be eliminated. Generally, if a question is not related to important job duties, skills, and work behaviors and attributes, it should not be asked.

It is not against the law for you to provide this information to prospective employers, but you are certainly under no obligation to do so.

Hot Tip: When arranging an interview, use your head. Do not accept an invitation to meet in a hotel room or any other secluded location where you might be vulnerable. You may know the company, but you don't know your interviewer. Be safe.

ASKING A FEW QUESTIONS OF YOUR OWN

A former New Mexico State University student described an interview situation for which she was prepared to answer just about any question except the one and only question that she was asked: "So, do you have any questions about our company?" Just a warning: you should always develop a few informed and relevant questions of your own. If you don't, the interviewer may discredit your interest in the job and your knowledge of the company. You may want to consider asking some of the following questions:

1. What makes your company different from others?
2. How does the job for which I'm interviewing fit in with the mission of the company?

3. What is the greatest challenge, from your perspective, that the organization faces during the next year?
4. What are the core values of the company? Does it have a mission statement?
5. What do you see as the areas that most need improvement within the company?
6. What is the short- and long-term strategic direction of the company?

Note: The initial interview should not be viewed as your opportunity to ask questions regarding salary, benefits, or anything else that connotes "What's in it for me?" You should be prepared to negotiate salary and benefit requirements later. This requires being familiar with the salary range for the specific position for which you are applying. (You most likely discovered this information during your preinterview research.) If the issue comes up, do not avoid discussing salary, but try to get the employer to state what the company has in mind. If this doesn't work, and you must state a figure of your own, it is best to give a salary range. If the employer insists on a set figure, then you have nothing to lose by stating the top figure in your range.

Things We Haven't Mentioned Yet

APPEARANCE

Dress conservatively so you can let your personality shine.

—Anonymous

"It doesn't matter what I look like; they'll be so impressed with my accomplishments, they'll hire me on the spot!" Right? Wrong!!! No matter how much we'd like to think otherwise, appearance does make a difference in the interview. This does not mean that you should run out and invest thousands of dollars in plastic surgery simply to look better for your interview, but basic showering and grooming is expected. **Appearance is the first impression the interviewer has of you, so you want to start out powerfully.**

- Dress: What you wear serves as an indicator of who you are. In one survey, recruiters ranked clothing as the leading factor shaping their initial impressions of applicants. In addition, 79 percent stated that their initial impression influenced the rest of the interview (*Communications at Work*, Ronald B. Adler). The definition of "dressing appropriately" truly depends on for which position you are interviewing; however, a rule of thumb is to dress conservatively. It might be fun to wear a bright red dress or a funky tie, but it may prove distracting for the person interviewing you.

Before

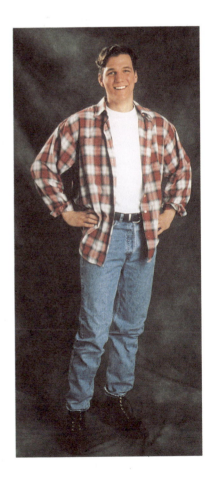

After

By dressing conservatively, you—and not your clothing—will be the main focus of the interviewer's attention. Suggestions for conservative clothing include a blue or black suit or dress, dark shoes, dark socks for men (not white—please!), and a simple light-colored shirt. Women should make sure that their jewelry is not flashy, and doesn't clank or make any other distracting noises. Men should wear a tie that isn't too loud and that doesn't have a pattern or picture that would divert the interviewer's attention. Use your own judgment, but conservatism is always your best bet. Save the fun stuff for *after* you get the job.

A common misconception is that you must have a designer suit in order to impress your interviewer. This is certainly not the case. Some employers take this as a sign of overconfidence. The interviewer will be more impressed by a clean, pressed suit (with all the buttons intact) and polished shoes. It is more important to look well put-together than wealthy.

- Physical Grooming: The conservative, crisp appearance does not stop with the clothing you wear. It is also very important to be well groomed. A well-groomed individual will be clean and fresh. Distracting hairstyles or makeup should be avoided. Also, a small amount of perfume or cologne is OK if it makes you feel more comfortable, but a large amount is not recommended.

SIX RULES OF EFFECTIVE INTERVIEWING

Rule #1: Play to Win

Even though a certain job may not be your first choice, you should walk into the interview as if there were no place else you would rather be. This is true for two reasons:
- You have the opportunity to gain a valuable contact and a possible source of leads to other jobs.
- The organization may unexpectedly emerge as the best alternative or as a potential employer in a year or two. (Never underestimate the value of networking.)

Rule #2: Make a Positive First Impression

- Say hello when you meet the interviewer.
- Make eye contact and smile.
- Shake the interviewer's hand firmly, but don't try to break any bones.
- Take your cues from the interviewer's posture and body movements.

Rule #3: Know Your Roles

During the interview, your roles should be those of detective, salesperson, and defendant.
- As a detective, you must find out what the interviewer is looking for before revealing all your qualifications and background. If the interviewer starts by asking you a lot of questions, turn things around by saying, "Before I go too deeply into my background, perhaps you could tell me something about the position and what you are looking for, so that I can keep my remarks relevant." You can never know too much about the interviewer's problems and

needs. The more time he or she spends talking, the better prepared you will be to respond to the company's needs with a viable solution: you!

- As a salesperson, it is your job to convince the employer that you are the best candidate available. Selling yourself in an interview situation can be accomplished in two ways:
  1) Indirectly: As the interviewer talks about his or her corporate needs, subtly reveal your own experience by asking intelligent questions and discussing how you have handled similar situations.
  2) Directly: You take control of the conversation by summing up your strongest qualifications. Remember, the interviewer is wondering why he or she should hire you. It is your responsibility to make that clear.

- As a defendant, you should welcome the interviewer's cross-examination and avoid becoming defensive, offensive, or paranoid.

Rule #4: Communicate Effectively

As a **speaker**, you should
- Maintain eye contact.
- Keep the message short and simple.
- Be specific; use examples whenever possible.
- Avoid mumbling.
- Sit up straight.
- Keep your hands away from your mouth.
- Periodically check for interest and understanding by watching the interviewer's nonverbal behavior. (Is the interviewer giving you a nod of understanding or a look of disbelief?)

As a **listener** you should
- Maintain eye contact.
- Listen carefully and attentively.
- Concentrate on the speaker instead of on yourself.
- Listen to the meaning of what is being said, without getting hung up on word choice or enunciation.
- Encourage the speaker with acknowledgment responses (e.g., "Oh, I see" and "That's interesting"), and also by asking exploratory questions (e.g., "Could you elaborate a bit more on that last point?").
- Paraphrase the question that you are being asked if you need more time to develop your response.

Rule #5: Respect the Interviewer

Common courtesy goes a long way. You should always use positive body language (e.g., maintaining eye contact, not holding a staring contest), use correct verbal language (avoid slang), shake hands, and stand when introduced, regardless of whether the person is older or younger, male or female. Never chew gum or smoke.

Rule #6: Respect Yourself

Keep telling yourself that you're doing well, even if you don't believe it. Avoid judging your performance, because after all, you **are** doing your very best. There will be plenty of time for self-evaluation *after* the interview.

Wrapping Up the Interview

In most situations, an interviewer will give you time to ask questions at the end of the interview. If you haven't already done so during the interview, display your knowledge of the company at this time. Ask about the latest product development, the company's philanthropic efforts, or its implementation of newly publicized strategies. This shows that you are interested enough in the company to learn more about it—you are going above and beyond the call of duty.

In addition to questions about the company, you might want to ask the interviewer questions about his or her career and the corporate culture of the company. You can then better determine if the company actually fits your personality. Use this time to reaffirm your perceptions of the company.

CLOSING THE DEAL

A commonly forgotten aspect of the job interview, and probably the most important part, is asking for the job. All the accomplishments and sweet-talking in the world won't get you anywhere if you don't close the sale. While the number of times that interviewees should ask for the job or express interest in the position is debated among recruiters, all agree it should be done at least once.

You can ask for the job in a number of ways. Here are two:

1) Sometimes the interviewer will ask at the end of the interview if there is anything else he or she should know about you. This is your cue to say, "I am really interested in this position. Could you tell me what the next step is in the interviewing process?" This continues the momentum you have built up during your interview.

2) You can also close the sale by asking the interviewer if he or she considers you to be a qualified candidate for the position. For example, "After learning more about the company, I know that I really would like to work for Hewlett-Packard. Based on what you have learned about me today, would you consider me a good candidate for this position?" This generally gives you a good idea of what the interviewer thought of you, and lets him or her know that you are serious about the job.

Hot Tip: Be polite. Verbally thank everyone you meet at the company who's been helpful in any way, especially such gatekeepers as receptionists, secretaries, and personal assistants. They are valued members of a business environment and often control access to the hiring decision-makers.

THE ARTFUL INTERVIEW

Some job seekers choose to use an artful approach in the actual interview process, so as to make themselves memorable and unique. One student at Johnson & Wales who was applying to a shoe company borrowed his roommate's shoes (made by the firm) for the interview. He commented to the interviewer that the shoes were comfortable, durable, and a great value. Many Johnson & Wales graduates also apply to The Gap's management training program. Of course, they make sure to wear clothing made and sold by the retailer at their interviews.

Chapter 7

Someone once said, "Success is where opportunity meets preparation." Stay confident. Stay prepared.

—Lansing Community College

The end of an interview is only the middle of the job-search process. Many job candidates mistakenly quit at this point, believing that there is nothing more they can do to influence the decision of the interviewer. Not true! A principle frequently forgotten by job candidates is that an interviewer is probably seeing many candidates for a particular position. After a while, even a conscientious interviewer who takes ample notes may experience a mental blurring of individual candidates. It is up to you to sharpen his or her focus on you as the ideal person for the job.

Follow-up of any kind
- Keeps your candidacy in high profile.
- Shows professional courtesy.
- Offers another opportunity to showcase your talent.
- Demonstrates initiative and projects an image of enthusiasm.
- Increases the odds of multiple interviews.

When you walk out of an interview, take a few moments to write down the following information in a notebook reserved especially for this purpose:

1) The names of the people who interviewed you and their titles
2) What you learned about the position, and whether you are qualified for the job
3) Any points that you forgot to make, or questions you forgot to ask, during the interview
4) What you felt went right or wrong, including questions you had difficulty answering
5) Topics the interviewer brought up more than once
6) Problems within the company that were mentioned in the interview that you might be able to solve

If there's a toss-up between two candidates, the one showing the most interest is likely to get the job. Writing down the above information will give you an edge in preparing an effective follow-up campaign. Although most employers expect a follow-up letter—the goal of which is to reemphasize your interest in the position—your objective is to give your prospective employers more than they expect.

You should send notes of appreciation promptly after the interview (many advise within 24 hours), because you will still be on the mind of the person with whom you spoke. Also, the longer you put it off, the more awkward you may feel about re-initiating contact with the person. A timely follow-up is also important because it makes a good impression on someone whom you should consider a potential member of your long-term network.

An important aspect of the follow-up letter is the phrase "thank you." Few people take the time to communicate their appreciation in writing. And you shouldn't feel limited to thanking the interviewer for taking the time to meet with you. Be more specific. For example, you can thank an interviewer for any insight or advice he or she gave you by citing specific examples of what was said.

The type of follow-up you choose will depend upon the position for which you are applying, your relationship with the interviewer, and your gut reaction to how the interview went. As you plan and execute your follow-up, however, bear in mind these final words of caution: there is a fine line between following up and being a nuisance, so be aware of verbal and nonverbal cues the employer may give. Hiring decisions are often made slowly. Be patient.

The Follow-Up Letter

Beware of mass-producing a standard thank-you note. Although you will always want to thank the interviewer for such basic things as his or her time or helpful advice, you should strive to give your thank-you note more substance. Now that you have the person's attention for a brief moment, use the note to jog his or her memory of your interview. Mentioning a specific piece of advice, or a contact name you were given in the interview, is a good way to start. People are flattered when you follow up on advice they gave you. Don't reiterate the entire conversation; just include a sentence or two that will make it easier for the interviewer to recall your meeting.

Rudi of State Farm Insurance interviewed a candidate just after having broken his wrist in a skiing accident. The candidate wrote a letter of thanks the next day, in which he included the sentiment "Sure hope your wrist heals quickly, so you can get back to the slopes!" The personal statement caught Rudi's attention, and the candidate was offered the job.

When engaging in business correspondence, it is best to use fairly conservative stationery. Although your Snoopy notecards were probably once a big hit, they may not go over as well with a prospective employer. If your penmanship is legible, hand-writing a letter may add a more personal tone to your note. But if your scrawl bears a close resemblance to hieroglyphics, a typed note may be your best bet.

Warning: in all follow-up correspondence, make sure the name of the contact is spelled correctly. A human resources manager at Sequel Solutions of Burlington, Massachusetts, was prepared to make an offer to a young woman she had recently interviewed. Before the offer was extended, however, the human resources manager received a well-intentioned thank-you note from the job candidate. The candidate's misspelling the manager's name cost her the job.

The basic format of the follow-up letter is as follows:

In **Paragraph 1,** you want to thank the interviewer for his or her time, and then make some specific mention of the interview:

I appreciate your taking time today [yesterday, etc.] to meet with me to discuss career opportunities in marketing [sales, research, etc.] at the X Corporation. It was particularly helpful to me to learn how the marketing department fits into the company's plans for expansion.

In **Paragraph 2,** you must decide the type of message you would like to convey to your interviewer. Are you interested in the position discussed, or do you have an interest in a different position?

- Interested in the position for which you were interviewed:
  I am extremely interested in joining your organization's marketing staff in the position we discussed. I believe that my education, experience, and enthusiasm will contribute positively not only to the efforts of the marketing department, but also to the company as a whole.

- Interested in a position other than the one discussed:
  I am extremely interested in joining your organization's marketing staff. However, I am more interested in a sales position than in one with customer service, and am hoping we can discuss the possibility of my working toward that goal.

Example:

Rebecca Smith
Dalts
140 East Wilson Bridge Road
Worthington, OH 43085

February 10, 1993

Dear Ms. Smith,

Paragraph 1: Express thanks and personalize the letter.

I would like to thank you for taking the time to interview me on February 9. I appreciate your being able to keep the appointment despite the terrible snowstorm that day. I enjoyed meeting with you and discussing management opportunities at Dalts.

Paragraph 2: Reiterate your interest in the position and remind the interviewer of your relevant skills and experience.

I am very interested in the management position we discussed, and believe I possess the skills that would make me an excellent candidate. As a waiter at Chili's, I have gone the extra mile to become a certified trainer in the host position. As such, I've developed a unified training program and conducted training workshops. I also strive to lead by example, conveying the message that every position in the restaurant is important and should be taken seriously. In addition to my restaurant experience, I have also had several internships that have enhanced the skills required for restaurant management, including

102

communication and organizational skills. All of my skills and experience can successfully be applied to a restaurant management career at Dalts.

Paragraph 3: Extend final thanks and indicate where you can be reached.

I look forward to speaking with you again, and hope that my candidacy receives serious consideration. Should you have any questions, please contact me at (303) 555-0138. Thank you again for your time.

Sincerely,

[Handwritten signature]
John Doe

Hot Tip: **Overnight delivery services can be utilized to get your follow-up letter to the employer quickly. This service also gives you the peace of mind that comes with knowing that your letter went directly to the person for whom it was intended—and when it arrived.**

Artful Follow-Ups

While many job candidates send quite standard follow-up thank-you letters (like the basic ones presented above), others send more personalized variations. To be effective, an artful follow-up must strike a balance between creativity and appropriateness. The objective is to present oneself as distinctive, unique, and the best candidate for the position.

Some examples: A student noticed that his interviewer had several books of a particular author on his bookshelf; they also had discussed the author during the interview. In his thank-you letter, the student mentioned his favorite book and noted similarities among the author's story lines. The interviewer found the student to be well-read, articulate, and sharing a common interest. A second interview led to a job offer.

In his thank-you letter, a student who was applying for a position at Disney mentioned several reasons why various Disney characters would want him on the Disney team. No appropriate openings were available, but the job candidate's materials are on file with the company. In fact, they're more than merely on file—they've been framed.

An artist used her follow-up letter as a forum to showcase her talent. Instead of a standard letter, she created a hand-drawn rebus that expressed her gratitude to the interviewer, as well as her ambition to join the company. It was obvious to the employer that the artist had spent many hours composing and drawing her letter, which helped to put her a step ahead of other applicants. While most students are not preparing to enter the art world, they should not ignore the follow-up as an opportunity to display their skills and enthusiasm for the company.

The Follow-Up Phone Call

The phone is also a useful tool in maintaining contact after an interview. If you have interviewed for a job and haven't heard from the company in a week or so, it is certainly appropriate to call and check on the status of the position. You could politely ask whether you should send any additional information, or when you can expect to learn of their decision. This contact conveys your interest to the employer and shows that you are still pursuing the position. You cannot always assume that the employer will be the one to call you.

Hot Tip: **The best time to make telephone contact without interrupting the business day or engaging in "phone tag" is either bright and early (8:00 A.M.–9:30 A.M.) or after the close of the business day. Strategic timing may increase your chances of reaching the person with whom you wish to speak.**

If you do happen to develop a close relationship with the employer's voice-mail service, don't take it personally! Most likely, he or she is not intentionally avoiding you but may be tied up with other important business. Be politely persistent, and you'll eventually get through!

Long-Term Follow-Up

Some hiring decisions take longer than others. If your interviewer informed you that the process would be lengthy, you should make an extra effort during the following weeks (or months) to keep your name top-of-mind among the people with whom you met. In addition to the standard follow-up letters or phone calls, another approach is to clip articles that you believe the interviewer will find to be of professional or personal interest. These can then be sent to the decision-maker with a brief note. The courtesy and effort on your part will be appreciated.

Keeping your name at the forefront of a decision-maker's mind can be accomplished in a number of tactful ways:

- Invite a representative of the company to speak to an organization to which you belong. This affords the company an opportunity to do some self-promoting, while also giving you the chance to further your networking.
- Attend lectures and events that are sponsored by the company. Speak to people at all levels of the organization. The more people you know, the better chance you have of standing out in the sea of interviewees.
- If you are involved in a class project that necessitates interaction with an outside company, try to involve the decision-makers at companies with which you are interviewing. A good example would be an assignment in your venture capitalism class to conduct reality-based market research for a new company product. Not only will you stay in contact with the company, but you will also demonstrate the benefit you can bring to the company—before you're even hired!

Chapter 8

Learning from Rejection

STOP

"I'm sorry, but we don't feel that there's a fit between you and our company at this time. Good luck in your job search."

"We'll have to think about it and let you know."

"We hope you find an organization whose requirements more closely match your traits."

"We've decided to hire someone who's interned with us in the past. I'm sorry."

"Thank you for showing an interest in our company. We'll keep your résumé on file."

"Your résumé looks fine, but some of our interviewers were put off by your lack of enthusiasm. We're sorry, but we don't think it would be wise to hire you at this time."

"We're going to keep looking, and we'll call you in a couple of weeks."

"We have concluded that your background does not match our requirements as closely as we would like. As a result, we are unable to offer you a position."

"Your background and credentials are impressive. Unfortunately, we are not in a position to extend an offer to you at this time."

"We're looking for someone who's got that special 'something' that's hard to put into words. I'm afraid you just don't have it."

Ouch. That hurts. Ten rejections. Just like that. And those letters and comments weren't even directed at you. They are, however, excerpts from rejection letters and explanatory phone calls received by one recent grad who, believe it or not, did pick up the pieces and go on to find a job. If you think starting the job search was a painful process, wait until you're faced with the prospect of continuing it, despite having received your own collection of rejection letters.

When students or recent graduates begin a serious job search, confidence and self-esteem tend to be very high. You are on top of the world! Obtaining a college degree is a very demanding and rigorous goal. Your dream job may not be easy to find, however, because there is a strong relationship between the worth of something and how hard it is to get. Remember studying the relationship between supply and demand in econ 101? As supply (of good jobs) goes down, the price (effort required to get such a job) goes up. The more desirable a job, the more difficult it is to obtain it. As a result, rejection is inevitable even for the most talented and capable of job seekers; the first thing you must realize is that it happens to everyone. If you've given a particular job opportunity all you've got, and the answer is still no, don't fall into the trap of equating rejection with failure.

As a recent graduate looking for your first "real job," expect to encounter rejection in the form of résumés unacknowledged, phone calls not returned, and interviews that lead nowhere. Resolve to learn from rejection, and remember that you will most likely hear a lot of no's on the way to the right yes.

It's a good idea to prepare yourself for the "n" word before rejection rears its ugly head. Use the following five methods to steel yourself against the dreaded "Thank you for your interest, but . . .":

1) Rely on your friends and family as a support group. If you isolate yourself during your job search, rejection will be much harder to handle and put into proper perspective.

2) Don't take rejection too personally. Companies are looking for a proper match, and while rejection may be unpleasant, it may ensure your happiness as well as theirs.

3) Hold "Ugly Rejection Letter Contests," such as the one conducted at the University of Virginia's McIntire School of Commerce. It'll keep you laughing and help you to realize that you're far from alone. (Rejection letters also make good dart boards.)

4) Look into job-search clubs that may have formed in your area. These afford people an open forum in which to whine, complain, and share their experiences with others. They're also a good place to network and pick up job-search tips.

5) Maintain a healthy level of self-esteem by putting the job-search process in perspective. No matter how well you perform in an interview situation, would-be employers may be basing their decision on factors over which you have no control. Your first "real" job is waiting out there; it just takes some people a little longer than others to connect with it. If you allow your self-esteem to suffer, you will communicate this to employers and ruin your chance of landing a job. Nobody wants to hire someone who lacks self-confidence.

REMEMBER: EVERYONE MAKES MISTAKES; SMART PEOPLE LEARN FROM THEM

Don't think of rejection as a barrier to success; instead, view it as a chance to build up your strengths and eliminate your weaknesses. There is nothing wrong with indulging in a little self-pity when you get word that yet another dream job has slipped through your fingers. But after a 24-hour mourning period, it's time to get back on track. To maintain your job-search momentum, convert any anger or frustration—whether with yourself or the situation—into a positive force. By conducting an honest analysis of each rejection, you will be better prepared to make the desired impression upon future interviewers.

Most job-search rejections consist of either not hearing anything at all, or hearing something you'd rather not have heard. The following pages offer some specific ideas to help you deal with each of these situations.

Situation 1:
Lots of Résumés, No Interviews

What if, after sending numerous résumés and cover letters, answering employment ads, and utilizing your network—no one contacts you? The problem may not be you. (Whew.) It may be your cover letter and/or résumé. One Johnson & Wales student ran into exactly that situation. Consultation with her American Marketing Association adviser revealed a minor grammatical error in her cover letter, as well as a closing, "Very truly yours," that is not generally accepted in business. A counselor at her school's career development office found that the skills included on this woman's résumé were basically sound, but the language she used to communicate her skills was too casual. For example, the career development officer recommended that she reword "ran a cash register" to "responsible for cash and noncash transactions." Soon after making the alterations, she began receiving interviews.

Also, if you receive a rejection letter after responding to an ad, keep in mind that the company most likely received hundreds of résumés in addition to yours. If you are still interested, try to contact someone within the company who can be of help. The person in charge of hiring may have never seen your résumé, so keep trying. One thing to keep in mind is that a rejection letter is truly a rejection letter only when it follows an interview.

Although we recommend that you focus your efforts on a well-targeted job search, playing the numbers game may prove to be a useful way to battle a rejection slump. Analogous to gambling, this approach assumes that if you place bets on enough numbers, one of them is bound to pay off. In other words, if you send out as many résumés as you possibly can, various opportunities will arise. A Merrimack College '89 student played the numbers game and won big. Over a six-month period, she sent out 446 résumés (an average of about 75 per month or 18 per week), landed 27 interviews, and received nine job offers. From those nine, she was able to choose the job that was best suited to her career objectives.

Situation 2:
Lots of Interviews, No Job Offers

If you receive interviews but no job offers, take a close look at everything you wrote, said, and did. Ask yourself the following questions: "Did I send a thank-you letter to the person(s) who interviewed me? Did I communicate effectively during the interview(s)? Which of my qualifications do I need to strengthen?" As you complete each step of the analysis, always be conscious of ways in which you can improve upon certain areas.

Did you do everything in your power to increase your odds of getting the positions for which you were rejected?

If you answered "yes" . . .

If you have conducted an honest evaluation of your actions and can find no definitive reason why you were not offered a particular position, the job may have been offered to someone with more experience or more appropriate credentials.

Remember that in today's job climate, even those who submit a strong résumé or conduct a good interview will probably have to deal with rejection.

The reality is that your lack of success may have nothing to do with your acquired skills. Perhaps you didn't fit in with the corporate culture or personality of the company. In that case, it's important to remember that you'll be happier in the long run that you didn't get hired by that particular firm. Don't worry; stay focused. You will find a company that has a personality similar to yours. That company will recognize your accomplishments and potential and will make you an offer.

If you are rejected for a job you truly want, says a career counselor at the University of Virginia, remember that just because a door was closed in your face, it doesn't necessarily mean that it will stay closed permanently.

To keep the door open, or to learn how you can be more effective in opening subsequent doors, you may want to send a follow-up letter to the interviewer:

Dear Mr./Ms. Employer,

I have long wanted to work for X Corporation because of its reputation for strong customer service. I was disappointed, therefore, that I was not offered a sales representative position after my recent interview.

I would greatly appreciate any suggestions you might be able to offer me as to how I can improve my skills so that I would qualify for such a position. I also hope you will keep me in mind for future opportunities at X Corporation.

Thank you very much for any assistance you might be able to give me.

Sincerely,

[Handwritten signature]
Jane Doe

Another option is to call the interviewer and ask why you were not hired. To those of you who are wary of potentially rubbing salt into an open wound: they already said no, how much worse can it get? Don't be bitter or defensive when inquiring; simply explain that you want to learn how to be better prepared as you continue your job hunt. Whether you send a letter or call, your interviewer may only give generic answers to questions about rejection. But it can't hurt to ask, and there is always a chance that you'll gain some valuable insight.

As your job search progresses, you may also find it helpful to send updated cover letters and résumés to those employers in which you still have a strong interest. Eventually, one of two things will likely happen: 1) you will gain experience in a job with another employer that further qualifies you for your "dream job," or 2) you will discover that it wasn't your dream job after all and lose interest.

In the words of Henry Ford: "Whether you think you can or you can't, either way you're right." Whatever you do, don't allow a rejection to be the end of your search. Pick yourself up and give it another shot. BE PERSISTENT, MAINTAIN A POSITIVE ATTITUDE, AND PERSEVERE! These are all qualities employers look for in a new hire, and now is the time to show them what you've got.

Ask yourself another question: "Do I really want the jobs for which I have been interviewing?"

If you answered "not really" . . .

If you really do want the jobs for which you've been interviewing, you may be reacting to one of two things. The first is commonly referred to as fear of failure. By not putting forth 100 percent effort in your job search, you may be unconsciously setting in motion a self-protection mechanism that automatically gives you an easy out in the event of rejection. It's easier on one's self-esteem to say "I didn't get the job, but I didn't really try for it," than to admit that you gave your all, only to be beaten out by another candidate who was better qualified, better prepared, or better connected. Now is a good time to remind you to look upon your job search as an opportunity. You owe it to yourself to put forth your best effort. (If your lack of interest/enthusiasm is evident to an interviewer, be aware that you also run the risk of having that information shared with additional prospective employers in the interviewer's network.)

The second problem to which you may be reacting is outright schedule overload. If you're a frequent victim of the too-much-to-do-and-not-enough-time-to-do-it syndrome, you'll just have to prioritize your schedule to ensure that you have the necessary time to devote to your job search.

Finally, if you suspect that the types of jobs for which you have been applying don't quite capture your interest, you definitely have a little thinking to do. It is likely that your lack of interest in the positions is getting across to interviewers through signals, word choice, and an overall lack of enthusiasm of which you may not even be aware. Our suggestion? Go back to the self-assessment exercises in chapter 1 (Do not pass Go. Do not collect $200.) and try to discover where your passions lie. Maybe you weren't quite as honest with yourself as you thought you were; maybe you have discovered things about yourself, or your chosen field of interest, that weren't quite in line with your expectations. Either way, a reexamination of your goals should propel you in a direction in which you are more interested and, therefore, more likely to be successful.

Chapter 9

Managing in the Interim:
A Personal Financial Appraisal

Insights on personal money management provided by MasterCard International Incorporated.

Looking for a job, as well as surviving until you get one, requires money. Not every graduate is able to shed his or her cap and gown one day and report for duty the next. Until you find your first career job, you will need to map out a plan to see yourself through. Financial stability will help you to avoid the temptation to accept the first offer that comes along. It will also make your search much less stressful.

Consider the case of Robert, a 23-year-old graduate of the University of New Hampshire. Within two months of graduation, he had several interviews, two of which were second interviews. In addition, he sent out 50 résumés. Despite a diligent job search and a 3.5 GPA, Robert still faced unemployment. To support himself—and his job search—Robert worked construction jobs and waited tables. His take-home pay totaled approximately $250 per week, out of which he paid student loans, health and car insurance, rent, and living and job-search expenses. Could you do it? In reality, you may have to. The following section will assist you in developing your own plan for managing in the interim.

Setting (and Attaining) Financial Goals

An important aspect of learning to live within your means is setting financial goals that reflect your needs and/or wants at a given time, in their order of importance to you. Setting financial goals during your job search is a particularly effective method of determining how much money you'll *really* need to live the lifestyle you want most. A financial goal is no different from any other goal you set for yourself; it's a statement that gives direction to your plan of action and which gives you a measurable target that is reflective of your needs and/or wants. Your goal can be as basic as "meeting my job-search costs," or as frivolous as "establishing a 'mad money' fund for my post graduation celebratory splurge." Regardless of the goal in question, a financial plan must have two things: a time frame and a dollar amount.

Example:

Short Term Goal:	Finance job search, spending $1,000 or less for interview suit and other necessities.
Plan:	Set aside $100 a month from part-time job(s) for 10 months prior to commencement of the job search.

During your job search, and long after you've settled into your new career, you'll find that setting financial goals will help you accomplish three things: 1) identifying the things that are important to you, 2) uncovering hidden dreams and aspirations, and 3) gaining purpose and direction in your spending. And whether your goal is to buy a computer this year "no matter what," to buy a new car within three years of getting a job, or to pay off your student loans within 10 years, recognizing these financial goals as such may affect the career path you choose to pursue.

We know, you thought long and hard about choosing an appropriate career during self-assessment, and you're right: two months after graduation is a little too late to change your major from a liberal arts degree to one with a scientific or business bent. You'll remember, however, that self-assessment is an ongoing process. Having chosen a major, for better or worse, be advised that it's never too late to reevaluate exactly what you'll do with your major. English majors and engineers alike face questions such as whether to pursue a career in academia, with a not-for-profit agency, or in private industry. The BIG QUESTION, now that you're actually out there seeking employment, is this: given your financial goals, which are a combination of wants and needs, is the career path you have chosen going to provide you with the money you need? To answer this question, you must first set some goals.

When setting your financial goals, it is essential to categorize them as short-term, midterm (or interim), or long-term. *Short-term goals* are those that you plan to accomplish within the next year, such as purchasing tickets for a concert series, funding your spring break adventure, or buying a television. *Midterm goals* are those that you wish to reach within one to four years, and can include everything from financing your job search to buying a car. *Long-term goals* focus on The Big Picture (i.e., a time frame four or more years into the future) and may include such expenditures as tuition for graduate school or saving the requisite down payment for your first house.

To more clearly define your goals, it may be useful to list them in order of expected completion and level of importance, using a consistent format such as the following:

Short-Term Goals (within one year)

1) Goal:
   Plan: Total $ to be saved
             Time frame
             $ to be saved per month

2) Goal:
   Plan: Total $ to be saved
             Time frame
             $ to be saved per month

Midterm Goals (within one to four years)

1) Goal:
   Plan: Total $ to be saved
             Time frame
             $ to be saved per month

2) Goal:
   Plan: Total $ to be saved
             Time frame
             $ to be saved per month

Long-Term Goals (four years plus)

1) Goal:
   Plan: Total $ to be saved
               Time frame
               $ to be saved per month

2) Goal:
   Plan: Total $ to be saved
               Time frame
               $ to be saved per month

Whatever your financial goals, the most effective means of attaining them—and of determining whether they are realistic—is to create a budget.

Creating a Budget

Exactly what is a budget? It's a structured method of managing your money—and living within your means—during a specific period. Budgeting will help you determine the amount of money needed to cover such necessities as rent and food, while enabling you to create a realistic plan for obtaining the "extras" that you want, be it new CDs or a new stereo on which to play your old CDs.

Establishing a budget will help you to

- Gain control over your income.
- Understand income.
- Uncover personal spending trends.
- Stay within projections.
- Attain your financial goals.

Three essential steps in developing a workable financial plan are 1) evaluating your needs, 2) establishing an income, and 3) learning to live within your means.

Evaluating Your Needs

Simply put, evaluating your needs means estimating the amount of money you require to live. As a college student or grad seeking employment, you have basic needs that fall into two categories: living costs and job-search costs.

LIVING COSTS

To estimate your living costs accurately, it may be necessary to log your expenses for a month or two. Recording expenses on a daily basis using a worksheet such as the following will ensure that you don't forget to record an expense, while also enabling you to track expenses by category on a weekly basis.

ATTENTION, CREDIT CARD AND CHARGE CARD CARDHOLDERS: if you have a credit card or a charge card, be certain to keep track of expenses placed on the card as you make them, rather than waiting for the bill to arrive. Remember that during times of uncertain income, such as during your job search, you should proceed cautiously in your use of credit. It's not free money; it's a line of credit that is a type of loan, and you are responsible for repayment. By thinking of card purchases as money already spent, you will have a more accurate reading of your expenses and can better ensure that you'll have set the money aside to make the payment on time. Remember that unpaid balances are subject to finance charges, and the last thing you want to do is create unnecessary debt while in the midst of seeking an income. For additional information on the responsible use of credit during your job search, refer to "The Role of Credit" section in this chapter.

Personal Expense Keeper

Week of								
Expense Items	Sun.	Mon.	Tues.	Wed.	Thurs.	Fri.	Sat.	WKLY TOTAL
Clothing								
Entertainment								
Food								
Laundry								
Phone								
TOTAL								GRAND TOTAL

The expenses you incur as a college student are likely to vary significantly from those you'll incur as a college graduate looking for a job, or as a new member of the workforce. That may make estimating future expenses somewhat difficult, but give it your best shot anyway. For example, if you have been living in a dorm or at home, ask friends and family how much in rent and utilities you should expect to spend. It's better to have a rough idea of the amount of money you will need to support yourself than to be caught unprepared.

Although living expenses vary from individual to individual, and from life stage to life stage, start with a basic format, such as the one below, and tailor it to your needs. Remember: your goal is to include everything on which you may be required (or inclined) to spend money in a given month.

WORKSHEET A: Personal Expenses

Monthly Expense Categories — Your Best Estimate	
Fixed Expenses (i.e., expenses that will stay the same from month to month)	**Estimated Expense**
Car insurance	
Car payment	
Health insurance	
Housing costs	
Savings	
Student loans	
Subtotal	
Variable Expenses (i.e., expenses that may vary slightly from month to month)	
Auto-related expenses	
Credit card payments	
Food	
Job-search costs	
Phone	
Utilities (gas, electric, etc.)	
Subtotal	
Optional Expenses (i.e., expenses that you may or may not choose to incur)	
Cable TV	
Clothing	
Credit card balance	
Entertainment	
Parking	
Miscellaneous	
Subtotal	
TOTAL	

If the estimated cost of your monthly upkeep is intimidating, you may want to consider ways to limit your expenses. This is not an impossible task, but you need to be willing to plan ahead and make the required sacrifices.

Consider these cost-saving tips:

- An increasingly popular way for college grads to save money and reduce expenses is to move back in with parents or other relatives. This interim strategy is particularly effective if they live in an area in which you are seeking employment. If they don't, you may still want to consider accepting temporary work in your hometown until you have saved enough cash to finance a move to a location of your choice.

- If you're moving to a city with reliable public transportation, you may want to reconsider buying (or taking) a car.

- Adopt an antisplurge mentality.

- Find roommates to split housing costs.

- Learn to cook; some very tasty meals can be prepared at very inexpensive prices as compared with eating out.

- Buy in bulk; toilet paper, cereal, toothpaste—anything. The combined savings can be mind-boggling.

- Clip coupons. Watch for sales and find out where the best prices are.

JOB-SEARCH COSTS

It may help to think of it this way: you and your parents have spent a tremendous amount of time and money on your education. All of that money was an investment in your future—and so is the money you will spend on preparing to get your first career position. The expected returns of a great job are well worth the expense. One of the unfortunate rules of the job search is that you must be prepared to spend money in order to make money.

In addition to determining the standard living costs that were listed above, you should be ready to pay for the following costs related to your job search:

- One, or preferably two, good outfits for interviewing. First impressions are largely influenced by personal appearance, so it's wise to invest in clothing that says you are a competent and skilled individual. The second outfit will come in handy for follow-up interviews. Men should plan on spending between $270 and $420 on their interview attire, which includes a suit, shoes, tie, and shirt. You should consider it an investment, since a nice suit generally stays in fashion for years. Women face more of a challenge because of constantly changing styles. They may pay between $200 and $300 for their interview attire. Watch the newspapers for sales—you can often find great bargains. Your wardrobe choices will depend on the type of employment you seek. The general rule-of-thumb is to dress according to the existing culture at the corporation, or agency, or national park, or wherever it is that you hope to be employed.

- Portfolio or briefcase. This added touch will help create a more credible, professional look for people pursuing business careers. On the practical side, it is a convenient way to carry around extra résumés and your job-search notebook (for quick access when it's time to make post interview notes). You might also want to include such face-saving elements as breath mints or a toothbrush, as well as a candy bar for quick energy. Expect to spend between $40 and $200 on a briefcase. (Note: This makes a great graduation present. Drop a hint to Mom or Dad.)

- Résumés, cover letters, networking cards, follow-up letters, photocopying, and postage. According to standard quick-print estimates, each résumé you send out will cost you approximately one dollar (24 cents for copying the résumé and cover letter on quality paper, 25 cents for an 8 1/2" x 11" envelope, and 54 cents for postage). Follow-up letters will cost about the same. Networking cards can be printed for around $30 per hundred.

- Phone bills. During your job search, the phone may become your best friend, because it is essential for both researching and following up with prospective employers. Limiting your job-related phone calls for fear of running up your bill may not be the best approach. Instead, opt to cut corners elsewhere by taking cost-saving measures, such as eating at home instead of at a restaurant so that you'll be able to afford your phone bill. Long-distance calls to prospective employers will be itemized on your monthly billing statement. Review them carefully so that you can keep track of your job-search costs.

- Answering machine and voice mail. Your goal is to make it easy for an employer to contact you. If you don't currently own an answering machine, get one. There's no telling how many jobs have been lost because someone was unreachable; you don't want to add your name to that list.

  Arnold, a national sales executive for Ryder Dedicated Logistics, is no doubt typical in terms of how he responds to difficulty in reaching an applicant: "If I received no answer on my first attempt [to contact an interview candidate], I would probably give that person the benefit of the doubt and make two or three phone calls over a period of a week. If I got a machine or talked to a person, such as a roommate, I would make one phone call, and if I didn't get a return call, I'd feel they weren't interested in the position. If a person hasn't set up a system whereby he or she can get messages, I don't really need to talk to that person anyway."

  If you don't have the cash to lay out for an answering machine, or if your roommates have a tendency to listen to messages and "forget" to save them, consider looking into a voice-mail service. You should be able to arrange such service through a local supplier for about six dollars per month.

- Travel expenses. Depending on the geographic scope of your job search, you may find it necessary to rent a car or buy a plane ticket from time to time. Be prepared for such outlays of cash, and try to make the most of each trip by scheduling as many interviews as possible during a visit to any given city or region.

Regardless of the nature of your job-search expenses, be sure to record all expenditures and to file all of your receipts. Good record keeping can help you budget more efficiently. Moreover, federal tax laws allow you to deduct some costs off your job search. Contact the Internal Revenue Service at 1-800-829-1040 for more information.

Hot Tip: In addition to your driver's license, most car rental agencies require a nationally recognized credit card in your name. If you are under 25, you have two additional considerations: 1) only one or two car rental agencies will rent vehicles to people under 25, and 2) they will probably charge you a higher rate. Because company guidelines are subject to change, we won't name any names, but be sure to verify that you're eligible to rent a vehicle from your rental agency of choice, well before you need the wheels.

Establishing an Income

Having estimated your monthly expenses, the next step, obviously, is to determine your monthly income. After all, you must have financial resources before you can manage them. Managing in the interim between graduation and your first paycheck requires planning because it is a unique transitional period in your life. You are looking for a full-time career job but are most likely required to make ends meet with a variety of temporary positions until you find that job. In evaluating your temporary employment opportunities, be sure to keep your financial needs in mind. Consider the following suggestions:

1) Paid internships can be a valuable source of experience and income at this stage. Many companies will hire interns who are recent college graduates. As a graduate, you may find it easier to extend your internship into a permanent position.

A recent Stanford graduate, for example, worked as a paid intern in the radiology department of the University of Cincinnati Medical School. She not only earned money, but also gained experience and networked with individuals who will be very helpful in recommending her for admission to medical school.

2) If gaining an inside look at a variety of companies while earning some money appeals to you, consider joining a temporary agency. Temporary employment can provide a competitive edge because short-term assignments can turn into permanent positions. Retailers, hotels, accounting firms, and other businesses with seasonal cycles are increasingly interested in freelance and temporary help. The obvious allure for them is avoiding the expense of employee benefits; the obvious advantages to you are experience, wages, networking opportunities, and possible future employment. In addition, temporary employment doesn't always mean five days a week, so a person in the midst of a job search can opt to have certain business days free in order to pursue full-time opportunities. Temporary agencies are often willing to try to match their workers' interests with the types of assignments they have available. For example, if you are interested in advertising, ask that they consider you for jobs in that field.

3) Many grads accept jobs as bartenders or waiters, because these are a good source of money. By being part of a busy restaurant or bar, you will clear a good amount of money without waiting for a paycheck. You also may have the added advantage of keeping your daytime hours free to continue your job search.

4) Consider turning your interests into money. Whether you have special skills in music, art, typing, or even the cosmetics industry, you can earn money on the side. Options include giving guitar lessons, tutoring, or serving as a sales rep for a direct-sales company.

Although some temporary positions may strike you as being a step backward, (particularly if your college career was marked by career-oriented internships), any job you hold will allow you to demonstrate your initiative and responsibility (not to mention the fact that it will keep a roof over your head and food in your stomach). It is important to remember that these routes are *temporary*, so do not become lax and ignore your job search. Keep networking, even in your temporary jobs.

When you have developed a list of all potential sources of income for the duration of your job search, complete Worksheet B, below:

WORKSHEET B: Personal Income

Potential Monthly Income Sources	Your Estimated Income
Salary (after taxes)	
Additional part-time/odd jobs	
Savings account interest*	
Interest on stocks and bonds (average per month)*	
Support from parents/relatives	
Other	
Other	
Other	
TOTAL	

*Although it's ideal and recommended to reinvest all income from your savings and investments—in certain circumstances you may find it necessary to use a portion of this money as income until you find a career job. If you do dip into your savings, replace the withdrawn amount as soon as you are financially able to do so.

Learning to Live within Your Means

Next comes the simple part: basic math. Subtract your total projected living expenses (Worksheet A) from your total estimated income (Worksheet B). If your income is equal to, or in excess of, your anticipated expenditures—you're in good shape. If the reverse is true, you will have to make some cuts in spending or seek a more lucrative temporary position. In either case, recognize that learning to live within your budget will require self-control, patience, and perseverance.

The Role of Credit

For good reason, most people find credit to be a useful component of their overall money management plan: it's convenient, it provides a backup in case of financial emergencies, and it helps to build a credit history. As you strive to match your financial resources with your financial needs during the interim, it's critical that your use of credit be both wise and responsible.

For those of you who aren't quite certain, *credit*, in abstract terms, is a form of trust. Financially speaking, it is the amount of money at a person's disposal provided by a bank or other lending institution. In other words, credit is the use of "borrowed" money that is subsequently repaid over a period of time.

While it is true that credit introduces a degree of flexibility into your budget, especially when you are living on a limited income, it's important not to confuse *flexibility* with additional *income*. Responsible use of credit includes living within your means, as determined by your budget, and recognizing that you alone are ultimately responsible for repayment of your financial obligations.

An essential element in the wise use of credit during your job search is the ability to determine when, and when not, to use it. Say, for example, that you were called back for a second interview. Although you've been putting money aside for a second suit, you still don't have enough money to make the purchase, and there's no chance

123

that you'll have the cash in hand before your scheduled interview. Provided you have a secure source of income, using credit to bridge the gap between your needs and your resources may be a viable option for you, assuming that the suit was already in your budget. Using credit simply enables you to gain use of the suit before your bank account would have allowed it. The price of such flexibility comes in the form of interest payments, but by sticking to your "savings" plan in the months ahead and by applying to your credit bill the money that you intended to allot to the suit purchase all along, you should be able to pay off your credit bill in just a slightly longer period than it would have taken to save the money for the actual purchase.

What should be avoided, on the other hand, is using credit to purchase nonessential items at a time when your budget can't support it. That's not to say that it will never make sense to purchase a big-screen TV or a gold-plated Civil War chess set on credit; but you should probably hold off until you have the financial means to pay off the charge with a minimum of inconvenience. The key to using credit responsibly is to never accumulate a balance that you will not be able to pay back over a reasonable period of time. When that happens, you are using credit to support a lifestyle that, in the long run, you can't afford.

Though many people don't recognize it as such, credit that is repaid in fixed monthly installments over a specific amount of time is generally referred to as a loan. When credit is extended for an unspecified period of time and payment amounts may change from month to month, as with a credit card—it is referred to as a revolving line of credit. There are two basic types of loans: **secured** and **unsecured**. A **secured** loan, with which you will likely become more familiar in the years to come, is backed, or "secured," by such collateral as a savings account, house, car, or stocks. The collateral serves as security to the lender that the loan and interest will be repaid. If a secured loan is not repaid, the lender has the right to assume ownership of the designated collateral. In contrast, an unsecured loan does not have specific collateral designated as security. Student loans and charge cards are unsecured loans; a credit card is an unsecured line of credit. If the borrower defaults on an unsecured loan, the lender may choose to take legal action and place all of the borrower's assets in jeopardy. The bottom line: borrow only what you can afford to pay back. Don't overspend.

Two types of cards are available to you: charge cards and credit cards. When using *charge cards*, you must pay your bill in full each billing cycle. (For both charge cards and credit cards, a typical billing cycle is one month.) When using *credit cards*, you have a certain amount of payment flexibility. It works like this: you are granted a credit line, which is the maximum amount you can borrow at any time. As you make purchases or access cash, the amount of credit available to you decreases from the maximum amount allotted to your credit line. During each billing cycle, you can opt to pay the full amount owed, the minimum payment (as indicated on your billing statement), or any amount in between, depending on your financial situation that month. When you make monthly payments or pay the entire outstanding balance, the amount of credit available to you is restored partially or in full, respectively. If you choose not to pay off your balance in full each month, your remaining balance will be subject to interest or finance charges. The amount of such charges is determined by the annual percentage rate (APR) set by each credit card issuer. As with charge cards, typically no interest or finance charges are incurred if the full amount owed on a credit card is paid during each billing cycle.

Hot Tip: **Keep a written record of credit card and charge card account numbers, as well as the contact phone numbers of each issuing institution. This simple step will help to ensure your ability to report lost or stolen cards immediately.**

To extend any type of **unsecured** credit to you, an issuer needs to feel comfortable that you will manage your money and your credit responsibly. For this reason, it may be difficult to obtain an unsecured card, such as those described above, if 1) you have never borrowed money and, therefore, have no credit history; 2) you do not have sufficient income; or 3) you've had credit problems in the past, indicating to an issuer that you may not repay a debt as agreed. However, you may be eligible for a credit card backed by your own money, which is sometimes referred to as a secured card.

A secured card requires that you open a deposit account (such as a savings account, certificate of deposit, or a non-interest-bearing deposit account) with the issuing institution, or with another financial institution designated by the issuer. Although you cannot withdraw money from your deposit account while your credit card account is open, many issuers do pay interest on such accounts. A secured card looks like, and can be used the same way as, an unsecured card. You have a predetermined credit line (based, in this case, on a percentage of the amount you have on deposit), and each month you receive a bill listing the charges for which you are responsible. Because the card is backed by a deposit, the chances that your application will be approved are excellent, making this type of card an alternative for individuals who have been unable to obtain an unsecured card.

With a secured card, you are able to set your own credit line based on your deposit account, and you can control your spending by creating a limit that doesn't exceed your needs or ability to pay. Provided that you pay your bills on time and stay within your credit limit, you will be building a good credit record that may help you to qualify for an unsecured card in the future. When that happens, your deposit will no longer be needed as security, and you can withdraw the money you placed on deposit, as well as any interest that has accrued.

When exploring credit and charge card options, be aware that each financial institution issuing a card provides cardholders with a Terms and Conditions statement, which gives complete information on interest rates and fees (if applicable), billing cycles, and the cardholder's rights and obligations. **Read it.** These conditions are not the same for every card, and your needs should determine the type of card for which you apply.

As with other forms of credit, cards become a problem only when you spend beyond your means. When that happens, your balance and interest may grow to a level you can't afford. One way to avoid this problem is to establish a budget, as was discussed earlier in the chapter, and stick to it. If you anticipate that self-control will be a problem for you when it comes to card usage, leave your card(s) at home unless you have a particular use in mind. This should serve to eliminate some of the spontaneous, unnecessary spending that can make or break a delicate interim budget. The important thing to remember is to control the use of your card(s) so that you never charge more than you have calculated into your budget.

Hot Tip: There is a new kind of card that is causing some excitement as it becomes more readily available. Basically, what's happening is that financial institutions are making ATM cards more useful than ever, by adding a new service onto these cards that lets them be used to make purchases directly at stores and other merchant locations. For example, an ATM card issued with the MasterCard logo on it can be used to make purchases at more than 12 million places worldwide that accept MasterCard® cards, everywhere from grocery stores and gas stations, to bookstores and restaurants, to hotels and airlines.

There are numerous benefits to using these types of ATM cards: 1) You don't have to carry a lot of cash or hassle with checks. 2) Your purchase is automatically deducted from your checking account, so there's no interest. 3) You get a receipt, and your purchases are detailed on your monthly checking account statement, so you'll know where your money is going. Most of the time you'll sign a receipt, just as you would with a credit card. But because it's still your ATM card, sometimes you'll be asked to use your personal or secret code (P.I.N., or personal identification number) instead. All in all, it can be easier, more secure, and more convenient to make a lot of your everyday purchases with one of these new cards instead of cash or checks. This new payment card can go by a variety of names— for example, to name a few: super ATM card, money card, cash card, check card, debit card, or even banking card.

Credit or no credit, living within your budget may seem difficult at first. The following hints will help you to do so:

- To make sure that all of your unaccounted-for income isn't frittered away on nonessential items, it is a good idea to include "savings" as one of your expenses. The extra cash will serve you well when gift-buying season rolls around, as well as when your car needs an unexpected trip to the repair shop.
- Guard against binge buying. Don't ask yourself whether you want it, ask yourself whether you need it. And we really mean need. It may help to think of a somewhat frivolous item not in terms of mere dollars, but in terms of other things you could buy with that money.
- Don't get discouraged. Unexpected events do occur, and at times it will seem as though your expenses go up faster than your income.
- It also helps to realize that over time, your pay will most likely increase and your budget may not be quite so restrictive.

Finally, to ensure that your budget accurately reflects your needs, utilize a worksheet such as the one on the following page to periodically balance your actual income and expenditures against your estimated income and expenditures.

MONTHLY BUDGET WORKSHEET

MONTHLY INCOME SOURCES	Budgeted ($)	Actual ($)	Difference ($)
Salary (after taxes)			
Additional part-time/odd jobs			
Savings account interest			
Interest on stocks and bonds (average per month)			
Support from parents/relatives			
Other			
Total Income			
MONTHLY EXPENSES			
Fixed Expenses (*i.e.*, expenses that will stay the same from month to month)			
Car insurance			
Car payment			
Health insurance			
Housing costs (rent, mortgage)			
Savings			
Student loans			
Other			
Subtotal			
Variable Expenses (*i.e.*, expenses that may vary slightly from month to month)			
Auto-related expenses			
Credit card payments			
Food			
Job-search costs			
Phone			
Utilities (gas, electric, etc.)			
Other			
Subtotal			
Optional Expenses (*i.e.*, expenses that you may or may not choose to incur)			
Cable TV			
Clothing			
Credit card balance			
Entertainment			
Miscellaneous			
Parking			
Other			
Subtotal			
TOTAL EXPENSES			**N/A**
Income Minus Expenses = Net $			**N/A**

If your budget is on target, congratulations! If, however, the numbers reveal that your budget is in need of a little fine-tuning or a complete overhaul, don't despair. Reevaluate your estimated expenses and projected income to discover where things went wrong. Ask yourself such questions as "In what categories did I spend more money than I thought I would?" and "Did I make as much money as I thought I would at my part-time job?" Then, create a new budget that enables you to live within your newly defined means. Whatever you do, don't give up on money management: in a very real sense, you can't afford to.

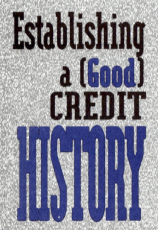

Establishing a (Good) CREDIT HISTORY

Your credit history is a record that indicates whether you pay your bills on time, how much you owe, and (by deduction) how responsible you are with your money. Three national credit reporting agencies—Equifax, TRW, and TransUnion—keep records of 1) personal data, such as address, marital status, employer, and salary; 2) your payment history with regard to major credit cards, department store charge cards, and loans; 3) inquiries made about your credit history over the last several years, and whether or not you were granted credit; and 4) as applicable, such public-record information as bankruptcies, foreclosures, and tax liens. Such records are compiled into what is known as a credit report. Your credit report is a historical indication of how you have paid your bills, just as your college transcript is an indication of how you performed in your classes. If you are beginning to feel as though Big Brother is watching, he is—at least when it comes to your financial habits.

A good credit history is important. Why? No matter how easy it is for you to pay all necessary bills right now, the reality is that you may someday need to take out a loan, whether for a car, tuition for grad school, or when buying a house. When determining whether to extend a line of credit or approve a mortgage, lenders look to your established credit history as evidence of your financial reliability. And lenders are not the only people who rely on credit ratings. Landlords may use one when determining whether to rent to a potential tenant, and employers may regard it as an indicator of your personal management skills. If you have no track record of success in the credit arena, you may find yourself more dependent than you'd like on your winning personality.

There are several ways to ensure the development and maintenance of a solid financial track record:

- As soon as you get your own place (with or without roommates), **maintain household services in your name—and ensure that all bills** (gas, electric, water, phone, etc.) **are paid in full and on time.**

- **Make student loan payments on time.** Depending upon the type of student loan(s) you hold, your payments could go into effect as early as the month following your graduation, or you may have the option to defer such payments until you find employment. Either way, make it a priority to find out repayment procedures and options a couple of months before you have to write the first check.

- **Obtain a major credit card or charge card** from a gas station, department store, or financial institution, **and make your payments on time,** according to the terms and conditions of the lender.

Hot Tip: If you are curious about your credit history, you can obtain a copy of your credit report from Equifax [1-800-685-1111], TRW Credit Information Services [714-385-7000 or 1-800-682-7654], or TransUnion Corporation [312-408-1400 or 1-800-851-2674] for a nominal fee. In addition, a new merged credit report called Confidential Credit is now available from Credco [1-800-443-9342]. If you have been turned down for credit recently, you are eligible for a free copy of your report. Should your credit report be incorrect, you are responsible for reporting any errors to the credit bureau. Accurate information—good or bad—will stay on your report for at least seven years.

Chapter 10

The offer is in. Do you accept it? If it's the only position you've really wanted throughout your entire search, and you have no question that it will meet your intellectual and financial needs, by all means take the job immediately.

If it falls short of the mark . . .

Remain calm and consider your options. If you receive an offer by mail, you can assume that you have at least a couple of days to get back to the company with your answer. If the offer comes in the form of a phone call, however, you'll have to ask for that time. Simply saying you aren't sure isn't the best approach; you still want the employer to feel that you are excited about the offer, in case you end up taking it. One way to buy some time, without negatively impacting upon future relations with an employer, is to request that the company put the specifics of the offer in writing. It should take a few days for the offer to arrive in the mail.

Now that you have the necessary time, get busy. In self-assessment, the most important aspect of determining whether a particular job offer meets your needs is to be honest with yourself. Don't try to talk yourself into something you don't want, and don't walk away from a job offer without giving it due consideration. The ultimate goal of your analysis, of course, is to answer the question "Is this really what I want to do?" Not forever, mind you, but at least for the coming year (the minimum amount of time that experts recommend you spend on your first job). In attempting to answer the Big Question, break it down into several more specific questions:

Will I be doing something that I enjoy in an environment in which I'll be happy?

If you aren't certain whether this is the position for you, go back to your notes on self-assessment, and cross-reference the realities of this particular job offer with those of your ideal position. How closely do they match? Are the significant differences based on long-term opportunities or the day-in–day-out nature of the position itself? Will you be challenged? Will you be given the opportunity to learn something new? Will you thrive in the company culture? You may also want to draw up a list of pros and cons. Putting things on paper can make them seem a bit more real.

Will I be making enough money?

The value of a job offer can be judged in many ways, and starting salary is but one of them. Nevertheless, one has to pay the bills. A standard rule of thumb is to assume that your take-home (or net) pay will be 65 percent of your gross salary (income before federal, state, and local taxes are deducted). Using information from your personal financial appraisal, you should be able to determine the absolute minimum that you need to survive after all bills are paid. (If you've been living at home during your job search, do you expect your new salary to enable you to move out right away? Or are you content to stay with Mom and Pop until you get a little money in the bank?) Divide your net income by 12 and subtract your minimum monthly requirements. What's left is your discretionary income. Discretionary income represents the amount of money you will have left over each month to do all those nonessential things like going to the movies, taking a trip, or buying CDs. It's also a good idea to stash away a portion of your monthly discretionary income in your savings account.

Benefits are also an important part of your compensation package and should not be overlooked. Having medical and life insurance as part of the job package may seem much like getting clothes instead of toys on your fifth birthday, but when you have to reach into your pocket and pull out the necessary cash every time you go to the doctor or have your teeth cleaned, you'll realize how valuable those benefits are.

Are there other benefits?

Does your employer offer tuition reimbursement should you decide to go to graduate school in the future? What is the vacation schedule? Is any flexibility built into the work schedule?

Is this the best employment option for me at this time?

Given the competitive nature of today's job search, it is extremely important that you evaluate job offers carefully, not only in relation to what a particular job offers, but also by measuring the ways in which a particular job compares with other options available to you at a given time. Are you expecting other offers, or is this the first glimmer of hope following a too-painful-to-be-remembered string of rejections? Are you weary of the job search? Or do you feel you've just now gotten the hang of it?

If you feel that you would prefer one or two other positions for which you have interviewed, use this time to get in touch with your contacts at the other companies. Your best bet is to be straight with them about the reason for your call and what you hope to learn. You might begin by saying something like this: "To be honest, I'm calling because I've recently been offered a position, but I'm more interested in the [title] position with [name of company]. I'm wondering whether you have any insight as to when that position is expected to be filled." This approach serves two purposes: 1) it makes your company contact aware of your situation, and 2) it gives him or her an opportunity to let you know about your chances with the company.

By analyzing your competing opportunities fully, you'll have a clearer idea of what this job opportunity really means.

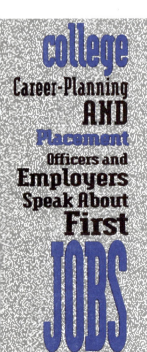

college
Career-Planning
AND
Placement
Officers and
Employers
Speak About
First
JOBS

Which of the following is most important in a first job?

Great experience/responsibility	86.6%
Great name of company or employer	1.5%
Great salary	.8%

How long should a college graduate typically plan to spend at his/her first job?

Two to three years	55.6%
One or two years	24.0%
More than three years	14.0%
One year or less	2.3%

Do you think it's better for a student to take a six-month temporary position in a second-choice industry, or to continue looking for a permanent job full-time?

Take a temporary position	75.9%
Continue looking	8.6%

Note: The sum of the percentages will not equal 100 because some participants chose not to respond to a particular question.

Source: MasterCard International survey of 429 College Career-Planning and Placement Officers and 183 Employers (September 1993).

Chapter 11

Congratulations! Now you can relax and enjoy the fruits of a job search well done. Well . . . almost.

Surviving the Transition

If this is your first "real" job, expect to go through the normal college-to-work adjustment period. It can be a tough transition from the world of academia, in which you are your own boss, to the world of work, in which you are expected to play by someone else's rules. No matter how beautiful the weather is, you no longer have the freedom to decide to spend the day at the park instead of at work. In most companies, you won't be able to set your own hours, even if your productivity is at its peak between the hours of midnight and 4:00 A.M. And you will almost certainly be expected to be pleasant to superiors, coworkers, or clients whom you don't particularly like or respect. Take comfort in the fact that everyone goes through a transition period; it's just that some people experience a more difficult transition than others. So before you make any drastic decisions in relation to your specific job, be sure that you've given yourself adequate time to adjust to the work experience in general.

On the other hand, you may find that you genuinely dislike what you are doing. How could that be? You researched the company's history, you talked to current employees, you got along with each of the interviewers. Hello. You have just come face-to-face with an inherent problem in the job search: there's no way to know what a position is really like until you take it. Secondhand knowledge is no substitute for firsthand experience. Most likely, you based your decision to accept a certain position on a preconceived notion of what life as a professional so-and-so would be like. After the luxury of an insider's look at your so-called dream job, however, you may decide that it's not what you want at all. And that's OK. After you've given your new job or career a fair trial, don't be afraid to change your mind.

Joe, who graduated from Georgetown School of Business with a B.S. in accounting in 1992, was very confident that he wanted to pursue work in the fast-paced, high-pressure environment of Wall Street. After a series of interviews during his senior year, Joe was offered his dream job: a position with a major investment bank. Unfortunately, the fantastic salary and prestige that came with the job were not enough to compensate for the long hours of work (80+ per week) and his inability to have a social life. Joe's "ideal job" turned out to be a poor match with his desired lifestyle and personal values. After six months on the job, Joe decided to opt for a nine-to-five position in his hometown of St. Louis as an accountant. He is much happier now that his career complements the lifestyle he prefers.

Making the Most of Professional Employment

The culmination of the job search should not be used as an excuse to stop focusing on your professional development. A career is neither your first job, nor your last. Your career is a combination of all your working and academic experiences, usually focused in one particular field.

Professional development is more than getting a job; it is striving for continuous improvement, constantly seeking knowledge, and focusing on the future. The more you work on your development, the easier it will be to market yourself in your next job search, whether it be two or 30 years from now.

Remember these points as you embark upon your career:

- **Don't burn bridges.** The first day of your career is like the first day of college. Few people know you, but you probably haven't made any enemies either. A word to the wise: the professional world of any given industry is smaller than you think, and bad blood could come back to haunt you later in your career. You've got a clean slate—keep it that way.
- **Develop new goals.** With a new job and environment come new challenges and desires. Set new goals for yourself, and plan accordingly to develop your career.
- **Continue networking.** You can never know too many people. Think of people as sources of information and advice. Regardless of whether the relationship is business or personal, personal contacts are essential to success in your career.
- **Keep current.** Read and learn as much as you can about growing and declining industries, current events that might affect you or your job, new or revised laws and regulations, and other information regarding your environment. Self-education will prevent you from isolating yourself in your work environment.
- **Develop new skills.** Take classes at night or on weekends to help you develop new skills—or brush up on old ones. (Incidentally, this is a great way to meet other young professionals if your job requires that you relocate to an unfamiliar city.) Many employers also provide in-house training for their employees. In addition to learning new skills, participating in such courses can also demonstrate to your employer that you are interested in furthering your education. Once you have mastered a particular aspect of your new job, ask your boss for new tasks and challenges. The more you learn about the company, the bigger an asset you will be.

Postscript

After reading *Mastering (& succeeding with) The Job Hunt*, good things began to happen to Kent and Anita. He was offered (and gladly accepted) a position in the youth services division of the city's social services department. Anita is now happily employed by Hudson Partners, an investment banking group.

What turned things around?

Kent: Following a long bout of indecisiveness, he decided to call some of the people with whom he had interviewed in the past few months. Surprised to discover that he had come across as shy and insecure in more than one interview, Kent began to refine his social skills and made a conscious effort to relax during his future interviews.

Anita: Reluctantly, Anita decided that she should reevaluate her career goals. In doing so, she discovered that the aspects of the financial industry that fascinated her were more closely related to investment banking than to consumer banking, the area in which she had concentrated the majority of her job-search efforts. Although altering the focus of her job search did take her back to square one in terms of researching potential employers, she was pleased to discover that a few of her networking contacts were willing and able to put her in touch with their acquaintances in her new field of interest. In fact, Anita felt so secure in her new direction that she turned down a position with a consumer banking institution and held out for the job she wanted.

Kent and Anita still get together at the pub—but now they hang out on the other side of the bar.

As you begin your job search, remember to

Be Positive,
Be Prepared,
and
Master the Job Hunt!

GOOD LUCK!

Appendix A
THE AUTHORS

Winner

New Mexico State University
Erin E. Baca
Donald Cordova
Clayton Einspahr
Mariah Garvey
Catherine Quintana
Kimberly Sais
Jason Sheldon
Kristin Tidmore
Kim Wallin
Paula L. Wheeler
Gwenn Wirth
and Dr. Elise Sautter,
Faculty Advisor

Finalists

Cleveland State University
Ghouse S. Adam
Michelle L. Gandolf
Gerald P. Jarzabek, Jr.
Ivan J. Kofol, Jr.
Michael Moon
Maureen M. Pallas
Zolt Seregi
Greg Tilton
and Sanford Jacobs,
Faculty Advisor

Johnson & Wales University
Brian F. K. Colbum
Michael T. Jones
Michael Ryan

Johnson & Wales University (continued)
Gregory Scott
Sheri Stone
and Cheryl A. Amantea,
Faculty Advisor

Merrimack College
Elise DelGaudio
Julie DiFilippo
Jennifer DiMento
Susan Iannelli
Doreen Lemay
Roseann Matteo
Julie Oriola
and Pasquale Vacca,
Faculty Advisor

Honorable Mention

University of Cincinnati
Greg Clark
Jim Earl
Tammy Schlachter
Troy Stiltner
and Frederick Russ,
Faculty Advisor

University of Colorado at Boulder
Erica Bjork
Timothy Ferriter
Christine Kaser
Diarmuid Truax
Broch Wutherup
and Donald Lichtenstein,
Faculty Advisor

Northeastern State University/
University Center Tulsa
Michael Hawkins
Peggy Hendrickson
Laura Hetsko
Jennifer Lawson
Jennifer McCafferty
Stephan Mecke
Anne Tenney
Barbara Thompson
KarenWhite
and Greg Marshall,
Faculty Advisor

University of Virginia
Steve Haidar
Karen Carney
Phil Manos
Lisa Yuen
and James J. Dowd, Jr.,
Faculty Advisor

Additional Contributors
Eastern Illinois University
Michael R. Anchuetz
Kelley E. Carrico
Joel D. Goodman
Dina M. Grube
Connie J. Helton
Aaron W. Kirk
Mark C. Lindgren
Matthew J. Lissy
Melissa A. Ostrowski
Jeanne M. Rakowski
Wendy M. Thompson
and Dr. Sid C. Dudley,
Faculty Advisor

Elmhurst College
Sharon Bragen
Donna Micus
Pamela Noyes
Brett Schulz

Grand Valley State University
Vincent Ferrari
Yoshiki Kumazawa
Jeff Sweitzer
Joe Walker

Harding University
Laura Adams
Tracy Childers
Daffana Gray
Kim Heffington
Richard Loh
and Charles Walker,
Faculty Advisor

Hofstra University
Steven H. Denker
Stacy L. Klein
Lorraine L'Huillier
John Nuzzi
Susan Surian
and Dr. Andrew M. Forman,
Faculty Advisor

Lansing Community College
Pat Bricker
James Stack
Vicki Stringham
and James Russeau, Chairman
Robert Ferrintino,
Faculty Advisor
William Motz,
Faculty Advisor

Loyola University, New Orleans
Michael Mullaly
Laura A. Young
Christopher Shea
Pat Donovan
Denisse Rodriguez
Tammy Angelety
Rina Paguaga
Michelle M. Pijuan
Harold Werling, II
Jennifer L. French
Symbol S. Schafer

Loyola University, New Orleans (continued)
   Elena Luz Mora
   Valeria Sol
   and Caroline M. Fisher,
   Faculty Advisor

Missouri Western State College
   Kim Cariddi
   Paula Eckart
   Jean Gloggner
   Heather Lathrop
   Mickey Mayes
   Robert Morrison
   Marshan Purnell
   Danielle Romine
   Mike Washburn
   and Dr. Sharon Wagner,
   Faculty Advisor

Ohio University
   Mike Baker
   Liz Blair
   Tom McCoy
   Megan McQuillen
   Sheila Snelling
   Kelly Vandall

Oral Roberts University
   Daniel B. Chaboya
   Sarah S. Freeman
   Natalie L. Nantes
   Martin A. Ruiz
   and Dr. Mark Maynard,
   Faculty Advisor

Shippensburg University
   Tut Bailey
   Kayleen Berry
   Elizabeth Dunkin
   Sherry Elliott
   Matt Pyfe
   Cory Hillis
   Lisa Hite

Shippensburg University (continued)
   Rachel Holthaus
   Matt Mundorf
   Brian Parker
   Ed Pines
   Allison Shriner
   Stacey Smith
   Karen Snoke
   Gabe Testa
   Susan Touw
   and Dr. Lynn Harris,
   Faculty Advisor

Southern Illinois
University at Carbondale
   Brad Denz
   Tom Harris
   Michael Jessup
   Peck Kuan Lee
   Jeff McIntire
   Kimberly Rinehart
   Leonard Vance
   Veronica Woods
   and Dr. Janis E. Brandt,
   Faculty Advisor

State University of
New York College at New Paltz
   Cindy Antonucci
   Amy Eienenfeld
   Elizabeth Davis
   Barbara Francis
   Jeannette Klepp
   Stephanie Leder
   and Theodore Clark,
   Faculty Advisor

Texas Lutheran College
   John Mark Brown
   Kristin Ferreira
   Erica Reynosa
   Leslie Schlather
   and Dr. Ronald Utecht,
   Faculty Advisor

University of Maryland
Brandon Swartz

University of Northern Colorado
Darryl Berry
Cindy Brethauer
Heather Jacobson
Amy Kowalis
Shannon Lani
Christine Shaver
and Lynn Owen,
Project Director
Dr. R. Viswanathan,
Project Advisor

University of Pennsylvania
Grace Esteban
Stephen Bierer and
Professor Cynthia Huffman,
Faculty Advisor

University of Wisconsin-Whitewater
Chris Dierauer
Mannie Gray
Brian Kohlmann
Roy Parker
Jason Severson
and Dr. Arno Kleimenhagen,
Faculty Advisor

Virginia Polytechnic
Institute and State University
David Carr
Tom Cramer
Marla Jones
Greg Merritt
Carolyn Michel
Jason Pleasant
Mina Song
and Dr. George Franke,
Faculty Advisor

West Virginia Wesleyan College
Michael P. Bullock
Paul R. Harvey, Jr.
Jennifer K. Martinek
Marlin A. McKinney
Charles E. Miller
Tracy Mosher
Lisa M. Tanco
Andrew J. Tokasz
John S. Wilson, Jr.

Virginia Commonwealth University
Rebecca L. Bales
Alvin C. Fowlkes
Belinda S. Go
Laura K. Lynch
Karyn M. Martin
Joseph V. Nio
Howard E. McCoy,
Faculty Advisor

Appendix B

RESOURCES

Equal Opportunity Organizations
The following organizations are indicative of the types of support and information services that are available to minority candidates during the job search.

Affirmative Action Register
8356 Olive Blvd.
St. Louis, MO 63132
(314) 991-1335
Runs ads aimed at minority, female, and differently abled applicants.

Council on Career Development for Minorities
1341 W. Mockingbird Lane, Suite 412–E
Dallas, TX 75247
(214) 631-3677
Works to heighten awareness and employability for minority college students, and to improve career counseling and referral services offered to them.

INROADS
1221 Locust Street, Suite 800
St. Louis, MO 63103
(314) 241-7330
Finds business internships for talented minority youth, to prepare them for corporate and community leadership.

Minority Exploration Committee on Careers, Associated
P.O. Box 450
New Brunswick, NJ 08903
(908) 932-0699
Sponsors career expos that link minority candidates with employers.

For a more complete listing of organizations dedicated to promoting minority involvement in specific fields of interest, we recommend *The Minority Career Guide: What African Americans, Hispanics, and Asian Americans Must Know to Succeed in Corporate America*, by Michael F. Kastre, Nydia Rodriguez Kastre, and Alfred G. Edwards (Peterson's Guides, 1993).

For company-by-company specifics, consult *The Best Companies for Minorities: Employers across America Who Recruit, Train, and Promote Minorities*, by Lawrence Otis Graham (Plume, a division of Penguin Books USA, 1993).